# PENNIES TO
# GOLD

## HARRY CUNILL

ISBN: 1-4196-8706-9
ISBN-13: 9781419687068

Visit www.amazon.com to order additional copies.

# PREFACE

I want you to learn how to buy and sell money at a profit.

My goal is to provide you with a simple, yet effective, method of trading currencies. This book will save you money and teach you how to multiply it as well.

Although I wrote this in the United States, you can trade world currencies from any country in the world, through the amazing power of the internet.

This book and your computer must be used together.

When you first read through this material, it may seem confusing, but it will become clear as you make real, currency trades. As you follow the book, and trade, *risk free*, the information will become increasingly clear.

Your time is important and valuable. This book will get you started quickly, and save you many hours of research time.

Newcomers, to the currency trading market, often spend a lot of money for software trading programs. Often, they end up paying high monthly fees for information and are charged high trading fees. This book will save you the expense.

You have in your hands:

- A simple, and yet practical, currency trading program.
- A free currency trading platform.
- Free, real time, currency pricing, and trading information.
- Free, multiple trading news, sources, and information, to assist you, in your trading decisions.

All For Free!

As an added **BONUS**, Pennies to Gold is providing free, "**BUY or SELL**", trading information at the authors web site: **http://moneytrader.web.officelive.com**

Your eyes are about to be opened to a totally exciting, new source, of global investment knowledge, and income.

This Trading opportunity _will fit your schedule_, since it operates 24 hours a day, six days a week.

After a few pages, we will immediately use the internet, to start your currency trading education.

You will be on line, with your own practice account, trading the currency markets of the world, with virtual money.

You will not have any financial investment or risk.

Today people see a penny on the ground, and will not bend down to pick it up. This book will show you metaphorically, how <u>Pennies traded, can be turned to Gold</u>.

When you read and <u>apply</u> this book, you will see the value of pennies, in a whole new light.

To your success!

Harry Cunill

# TABLE OF CONTENTS

# WHY THIS BOOK

When I first ventured into currency trading, I never found a simple, step by step, trading book. This book will guide you, from no knowledge, to actually trading currencies.

This book serves that purpose. It is not a comprehensive, highly complicated manual. The basic information can be used immediately, to profit from a very complex trading environment.

My desire is to…

- Teach you a <u>global</u> investing skill.

- Risk free.

- Which you can do from anywhere in the world, that has internet access.

This book is going to cover the basics, of when to "BUY or Sell".

We will cover: Trend Lines, Chart Patterns, Moving Averages, Relative Strength Indicators, and "News - That Makes Money".

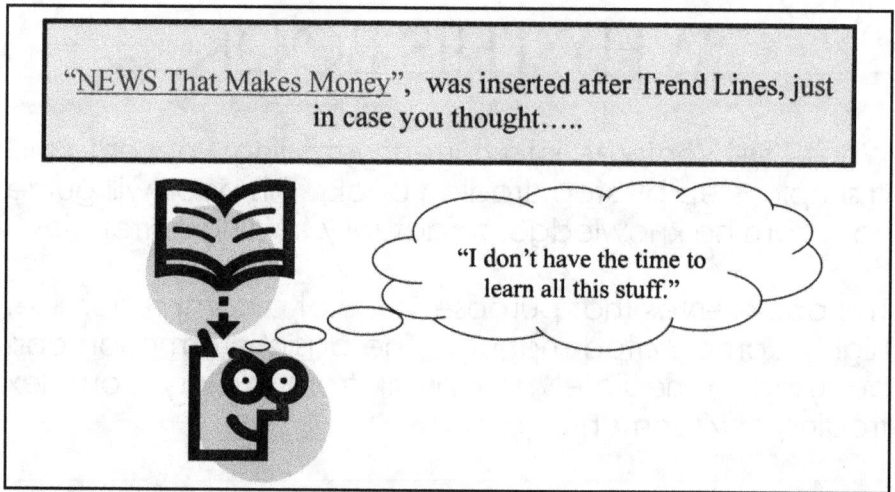

If you have 5 minutes per day, read the section, "**NEWS THAT CAN MAKE YOU MONEY**".

Use my news <u>trading technique</u>, as covered in this book.

Once each day, *Monday* through *Friday*, using the <u>news information</u>, enter a Trade order. Using the game platform, monitor your profits or losses for one month. I believe you will be pleased with the results.

*Never trade, unless you check the news first!*

If you make BIG purchases, your risk / reward will increase dramatically.

Always remember the story of the Tortoise and the Hare.

Always move forward, slow and steady.

# THE FOREX

**The Foreign Exchange Market**

The FOREX, or FX, is an acronym for the Foreign Exchange Market. Market places where one country's currency is converted to that of another. Without such an orderly exchange, there would be no global markets and if nothing sells nothing happens.

**"NOTHING HAPPENS UNTIL SOMEONE SELLS SOMETHING"**

When someone sells a product, idea, entertainment, or information; an <u>exchange occurs</u>. This constant (selling) exchange, like blood, provides life to the entire world. Where the exchange is at a minimum, poverty, ignorance and poor health are evident.

I often ask people from all walks of life this question. "<u>Do you know what the FOREX is?</u>"

Most people do not have the faintest idea.

Try asking some of your friends and see what they say.

Imagine, the clothes you wear, vehicle parts, appliances, electronics, and more, come from all over the world.

A foreign country, trading with the United States, sold items for dollars. Those dollars must be converted back to the country's currency. Without the FOREX it would be extremely difficult to exchange currencies or conduct international business.

If you asked your friends, "Have you heard of, or know something about the New York stock exchange?" The majority will be able to tell you something about it.

Yet the FOREX market is, <u>30 times larger </u>than the U.S. stock market, impacts the entire world, and few know anything about it.

If the stock market goes up or down, it does not impact every citizen. However, a rise or fall, of a countries', money value, affects everyone.

Global money managers, banks, and companies, trade in many different currencies. What happens when a country's money begins to lose value? Businesses will exchange a portion of their cash reserves, for a currency that is getting stronger. This action preserves the companies' capital and causes it to increase in value.

On April 26, 2007, CNBC reported, that the Dow Jones average broke an all time high of 13,000. Nineteen major US corporations reported higher than expected earnings.

The reporter's research revealed that on average, 48% of the corporations' earnings resulted from trading the FOREX market, and not from the products or services sold.

They traded US dollars, for currencies which were increasing in value. The companies not only preserved their capital, but made large profits as well.

Five percent of FOREX trading is done by companies and governments doing business with other countries. Ninety-five percent trade money for profit, literally making billions of dollars in the process.

**One Billion in One Day**

On Black Wednesday, (September 16, 1992), George Soros became immediately famous when he SOLD SHORT more than $10 billion worth of pounds, profiting from the Bank of England's reluctance to either raise its interest rates to levels comparable to those of other European Exchange Rates. Soros earned an estimated <u>US $ 1.1 billion</u> in the process. He was dubbed "the man who broke the Bank of England."

We are living in very exciting times because nations around the globe "sold something" and they are <u>growing and prospering.</u> As global selling explodes, the FOREX continues to rapidly expand, to the tune of 1.9 trillion dollars, changing hands each day. Consider that in 1977, the average daily exchange was 5 billion dollars.

The FOREX is open 24 hours a day, starts Sunday, 5PM, Eastern Time and closes Friday at 4:30PM, EST.

The largest FOREX center in the world is London. Other financial centers that follow the sun across the sky are; New York, Tokyo, Hong Kong, Singapore, and Zurich.

For the first time in history, the average investor now has access to this incredible market.

Regardless of your schedule, or time, you can trade this market!

# THE MAJOR WORLD CURRENCIES

As of this writing there are 6 major currencies which trade against the US dollar. It is recommended that you trade these six due to the high liquidity and sheer volume of activity.

Ease of liquidity and high volume means fast trades and low trading cost.

As you become familiar with the trading platform you can view the quote panel and see many of the world's currencies, which you can easily trade.

All currencies are traded in pairs.

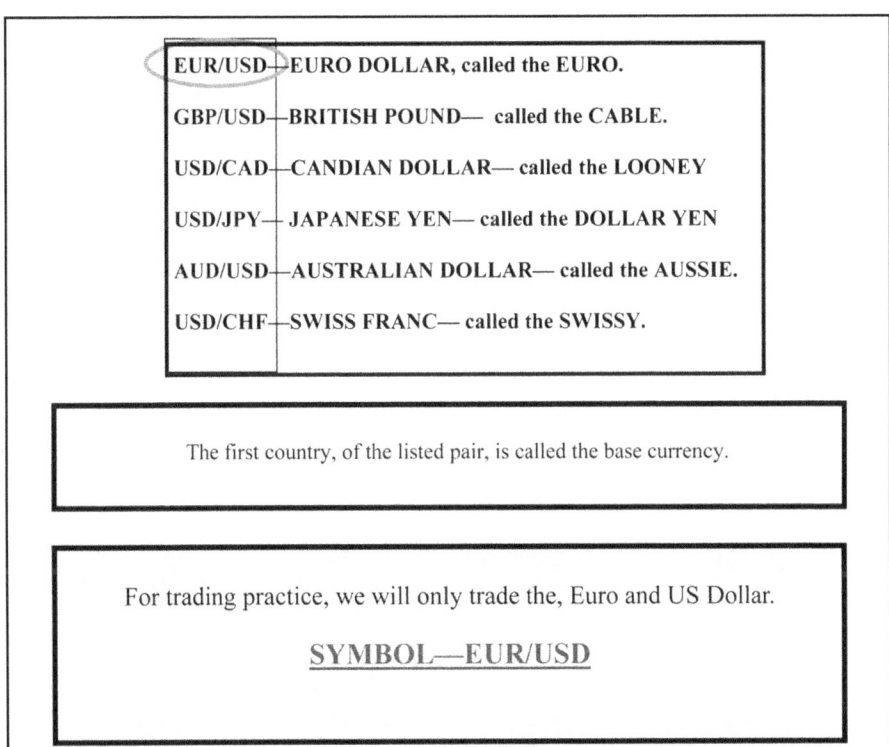

EUR/USD—EURO DOLLAR, called the EURO.

GBP/USD—BRITISH POUND— called the CABLE.

USD/CAD—CANDIAN DOLLAR— called the LOONEY

USD/JPY— JAPANESE YEN— called the DOLLAR YEN

AUD/USD—AUSTRALIAN DOLLAR— called the AUSSIE.

USD/CHF—SWISS FRANC— called the SWISSY.

The first country, of the listed pair, is called the base currency.

For trading practice, we will only trade the, Euro and US Dollar.

### SYMBOL—EUR/USD

# THE PIP

If you went to a bank and exchanged Dollars for Euros, you would be buying Euros, while at the same time selling your dollars. There is a higher price paid when you buy the Euro, and a lower price offered, if you immediately, sold back the Euro. The difference between the buying and selling price is called the spread and is measured in a term called, PIPs—Price Interest Points. The PIP will be very important important to you, since it is the measure used to determine if you are making or losing money.

The trading company I use has narrow spreads, allowing the trader to reduce trading cost. The average Euro/Dollar spread charged by Oanda is, 1.5 PIPs. When you log on to Oanda's web site you can read why this means more money in your pocket. There are many FOREX trading companies which, charge you more to trade and require you to make large purchases. With these companies you can forget trading pennies.

To most people, money prices have two numbers after the decimal point, example $1.35. They do not see the

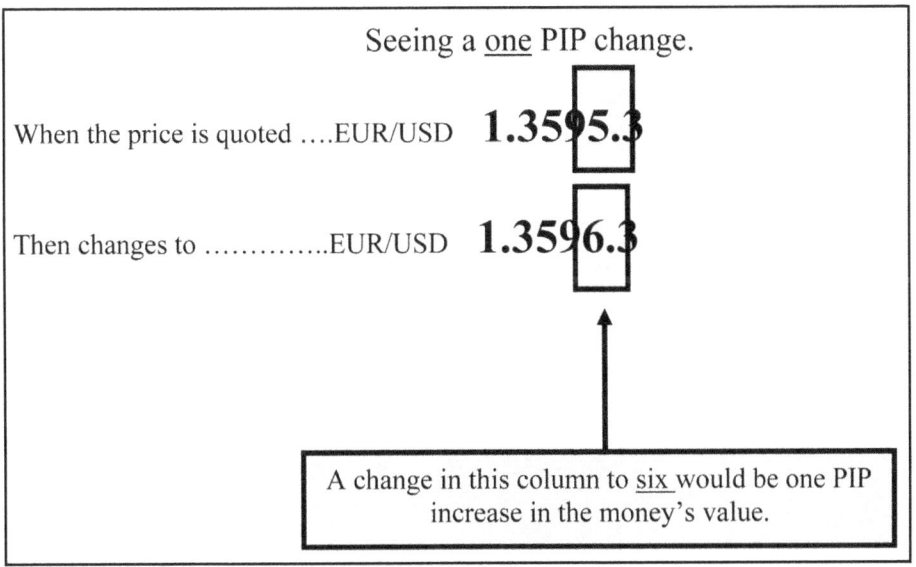

Seeing a <u>one</u> PIP change.

When the price is quoted ....EUR/USD **1.3595.3**

Then changes to ..............EUR/USD **1.3596.3**

A change in this column to <u>six</u> would be one PIP increase in the money's value.

next three numbers which are constantly changing in the major currency markets. Those 1/1000 or 1/100th of a cent, is where millions of dollars are earned or lost.

If you bought at 1.3595.3, and 1 minute later it closes at 1.3596.9, the increase in value would be 1.6 PIPs gain. If it dropped in price to 1.3593.1, you would have lost (−2.2 PIPs).

A minus sign (−) in front of the PIP number, means, you are losing money. No minus sign and you are making a profit. The trading platform will convert your PIPs, to its money value.

The <u>SPREAD</u> is where the brokers, "market makers", make their money, when a customer enters a trade.

It is the difference between the BUYING PRICE and the SELLING PRICE. There are no other commissions paid. Figure 1 shows a 10 PIP spread, typical for a Sunday afternoon, when the FOREX market opens. This wide spread is due to low liquidity, few buyers and sellers. By Sunday night, the spread narrows to 1.5 PIPs. If you entered a trade at this price spread, it would have cost you 10 PIPs. When your order is executed, a minus (−10) PIPs will be displayed. The currency would have to increase in value by 10 PIPs for you to cover your trade cost. If you enter your trade at, 1.5 PIPs spread, the currency would need to increase in value by only, 1.5 PIPs. The normal spread is 1.5 PIPs or less.

# THE VALUE OF THE PIP

Price Interest Points- shows your profit or loss.

Loss or profit is realized <u>only</u> when you close out your TRADE.

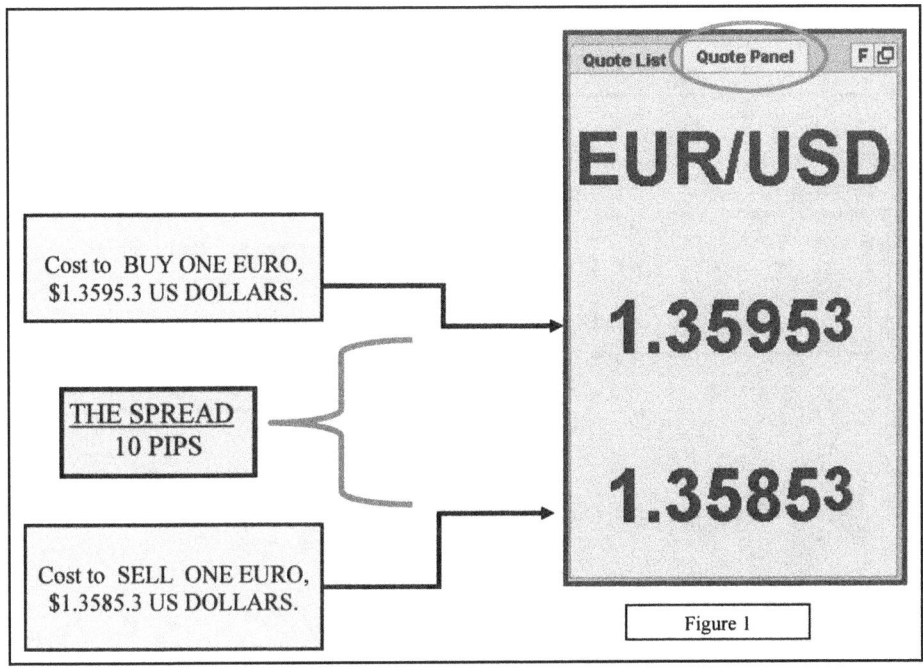

Cost to BUY ONE EURO, $1.3595.3 US DOLLARS.

<u>THE SPREAD</u>
10 PIPS

Cost to SELL ONE EURO, $1.3585.3 US DOLLARS.

EUR/USD

1.35953

1.35853

Figure 1

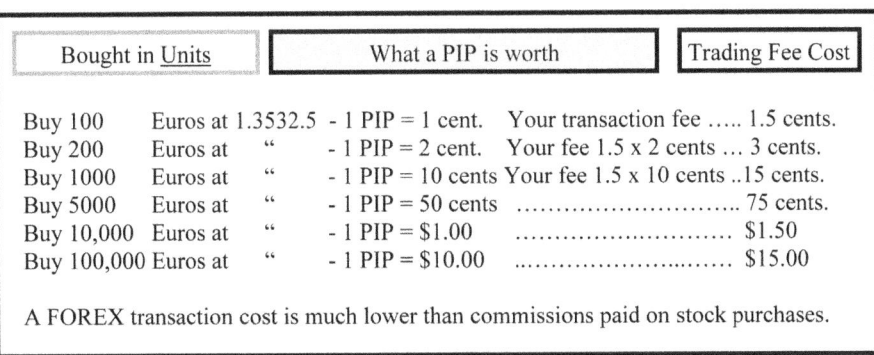

| Bought in <u>Units</u> | What a PIP is worth | Trading Fee Cost |
|---|---|---|
| Buy 100 Euros at 1.3532.5 | - 1 PIP = 1 cent. Your transaction fee ..... 1.5 cents. | |
| Buy 200 Euros at " | - 1 PIP = 2 cent. Your fee 1.5 x 2 cents ... 3 cents. | |
| Buy 1000 Euros at " | - 1 PIP = 10 cents Your fee 1.5 x 10 cents ..15 cents. | |
| Buy 5000 Euros at " | - 1 PIP = 50 cents ........................... 75 cents. | |
| Buy 10,000 Euros at " | - 1 PIP = $1.00 ......................... $1.50 | |
| Buy 100,000 Euros at " | - 1 PIP = $10.00 .......................... $15.00 | |

A FOREX transaction cost is much lower than commissions paid on stock purchases.

TRANSLATING PIPs INTO MONETARY TERMS USING OANDA.

All currency is purchased in UNITS. If you buy 100 units, you are not purchasing 100 Euros. Units are used as a measure, of the amount of currency, you are *controlling*.

As you can see, a PIP can have a value of, 1 cent, 10 cents, $1.00, or more. The PIP'S value is determined by the number of units you buy at the time you start your trade. If you BUY, 10,000 units, EUR/USD, and the Euro increases in value by 10 PIPs, you earned $10.00.

On average, the EUR/USD will move up or down in value, 65 to 100 PIPs, per day.

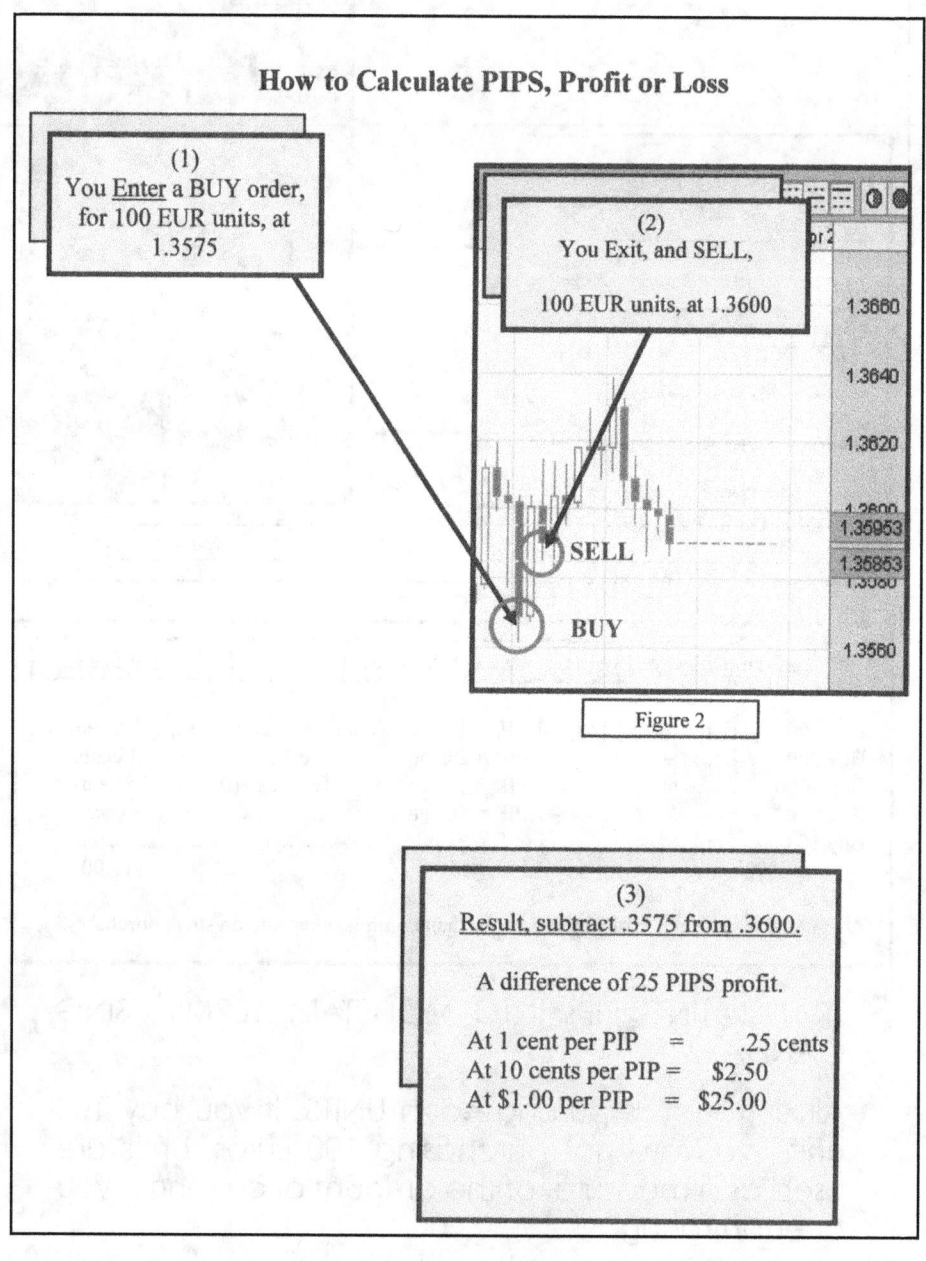

**How to Calculate PIPS, Profit or Loss**

(1)
You Enter a BUY order, for 100 EUR units, at 1.3575

(2)
You Exit, and SELL,

100 EUR units, at 1.3600

1.3660

1.3640

1.3620

1.35953

1.35853

SELL

BUY

1.3560

Figure 2

(3)
Result, subtract .3575 from .3600.

A difference of 25 PIPS profit.

At 1 cent per PIP    =    .25 cents
At 10 cents per PIP =   $2.50
At $1.00 per PIP    =   $25.00

# SELLING FIRST AND BUYING BACK LATER

A unique feature of the FOREX Market is the ability to ENTER a SELL TRADE first, and EXIT, on a BUY TRADE price. New FOREX traders often have difficulty understanding this concept.

Since we purchase currency in pairs, the act of Selling the EUR, is also the act of buying the dollar. The stock market does not have this feature since stocks are not bought and sold in pairs. By entering a SELL TRADE, you can profit from declining currency value, as well as an increase.

If you believe the EURO will decline in value, you enter a SELL TRADE, pay the SELLING price, and see if the EURO declines in value. You exit the trade, at the buying price.

The difference in PIPs is your gain or loss.

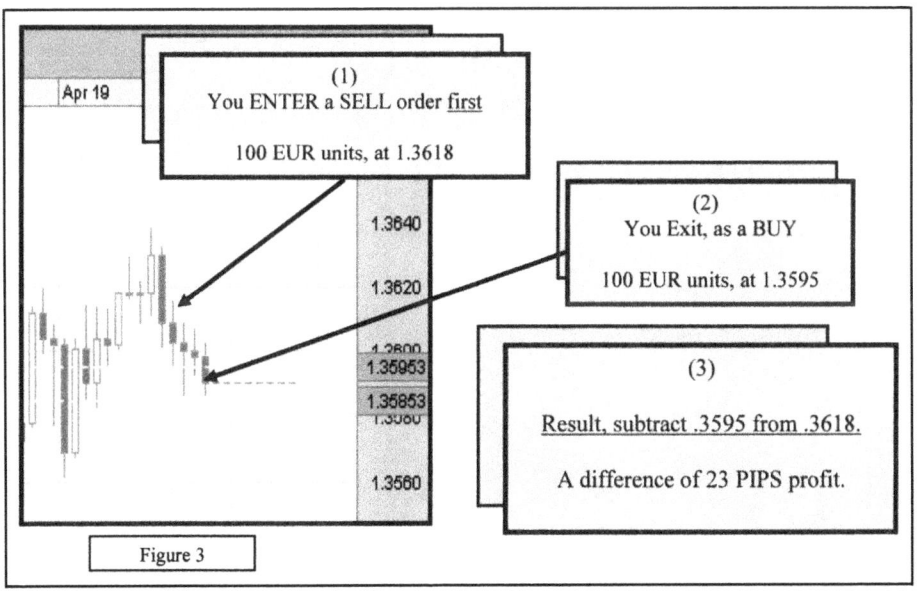

(1)
You ENTER a SELL order first

100 EUR units, at 1.3618

(2)
You Exit, as a BUY

100 EUR units, at 1.3595

(3)

Result, subtract .3595 from .3618.

A difference of 23 PIPS profit.

Figure 3

# GETTING STARTED

Very short term, the currency market can appear chaotic at times. However, major currencies will trend in one direction, for long periods of time. The money will steadily increase or decrease in value, over a period of months. In the dynamic world we live in, political events, world tensions, interest rate changes, and economic reports, will cause momentary, volatile movements, up or down, in the currency. These movements can result in profits as well as loss, depending on how you invest.

Unlike a stock which can go to zero in value, it would be a historical rarity for a countries' currency to do so. Countries change interest rates very slowly, to avoid disruptions in their currency's value. These slow changes result in long term trends of, increasing or decreasing value. A major currency is backed by the country, unlike a business which can be here today and gone tomorrow.

The following pages will guide you in opening a real time, practice account , without risking any money.

You will be using the same trading platform I use.

I am not affiliated with nor compensated in anyway by Oanda's corporation.

You can go to the following web site—http://www.goforex. net/forex-broker-ratings.htm, and read the reviews on Oanda. You can also check out other companies.

I have been very pleased with Oanda. If I make a phone call or send an email they answer and respond quickly to my questions. I can also make small currency purchases and yet receive the same conditions, information, tools, prices and execution as the large traders.

This book will provide you with other internet sites which can help you further your FOREX education.

As you gain experience you will develop your own trading style and preferences.

The next page will direct you to OANDA's web site. You will register for the game and login to the account.

1. Open internet explorer, use your browser or Google service, type in: https://fxtrade.oanda.com/ - click go.
2. At Oanda's home page you will find much information. Review it at your leisure.
3. After you register, click open, FX game, and open up a game account.
4. With your ID, and password, login to FXgame. If you have problems opening the program, confirm you have Java. If not, type java.com, in your browser and download the free java program. Java allows a computer to receive, real time, interactive communication.

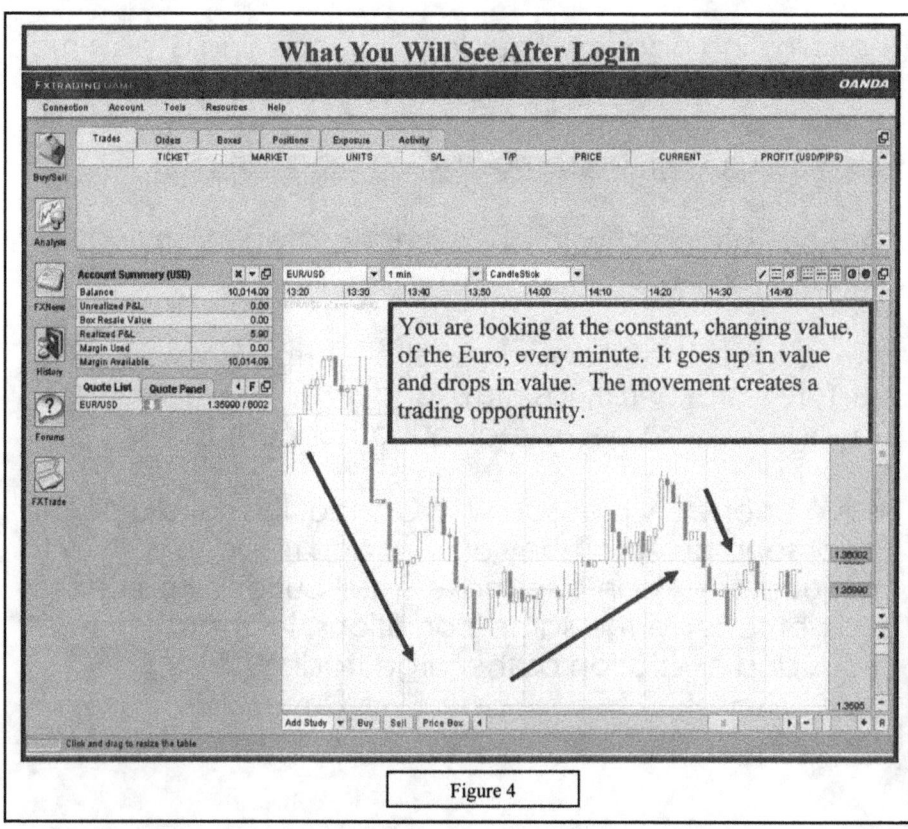

Figure 4

## How to Set Up Your Account

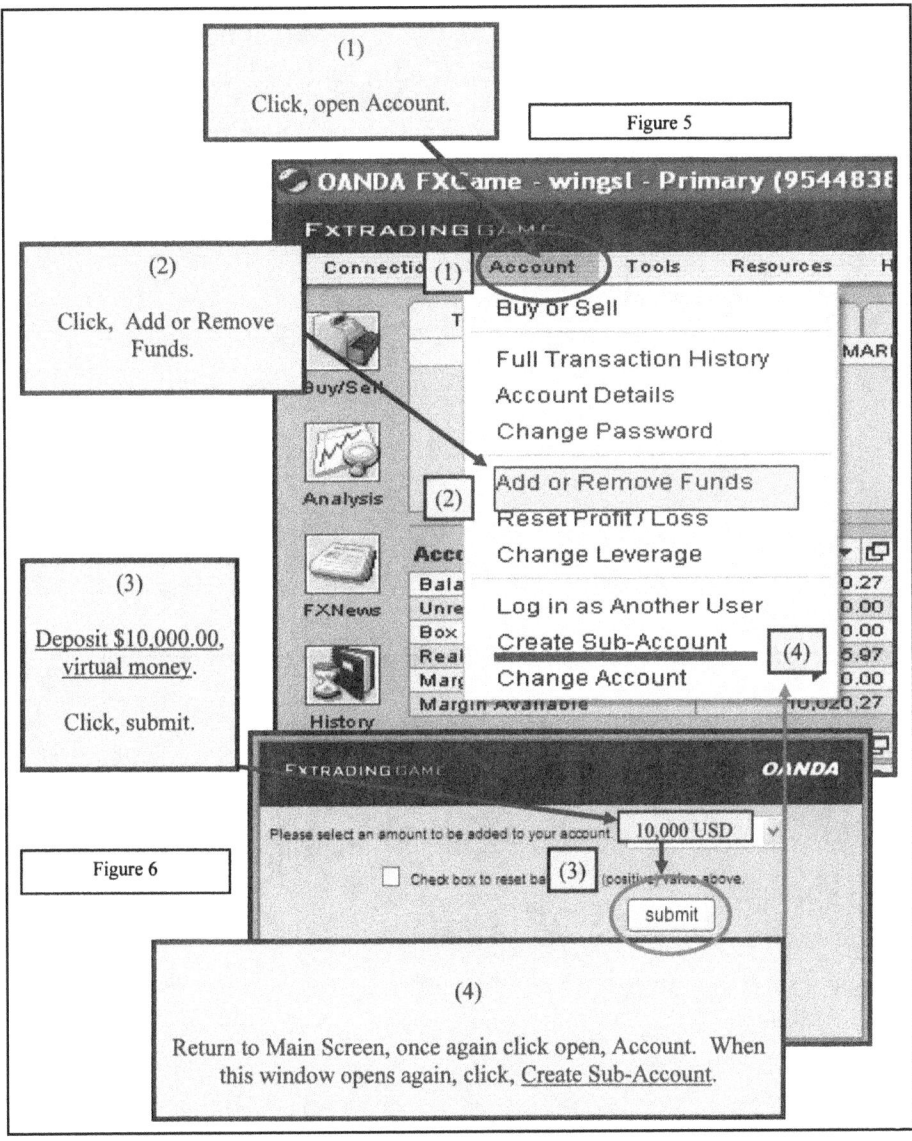

**(1)**

Click, open Account.

Figure 5

**(2)**

Click, Add or Remove Funds.

**(3)**

Deposit $10,000.00, virtual money.

Click, submit.

Figure 6

**(4)**

Return to Main Screen, once again click open, Account. When this window opens again, click, Create Sub-Account.

## Creating a Sub-Account

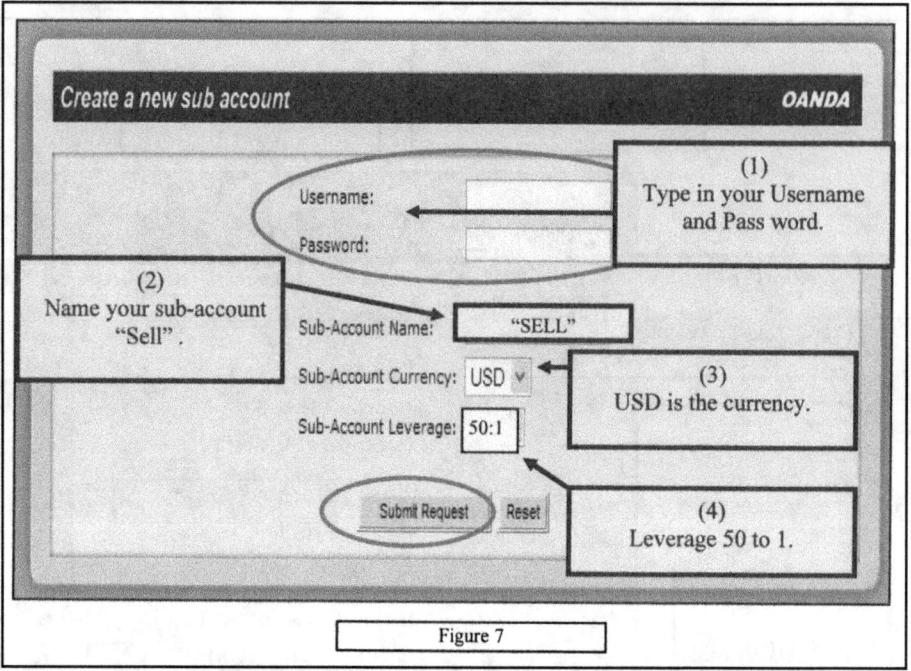

Figure 7

From Oanda's web site read the section on leverage. At 50 to 1, Oanda will fund 50 times your initial currency purchase as a loan, so you control more money.

Other FOREX dealers will do 200 to 1.

This may look very attractive, if you consider that $1,000 will control $200,000 in currency, but it is also very risky.

You will now have two accounts, one to enter BUY TRADES, and one to enter SELL TRADES.

Next we will add funds to the SELL, sub-account.

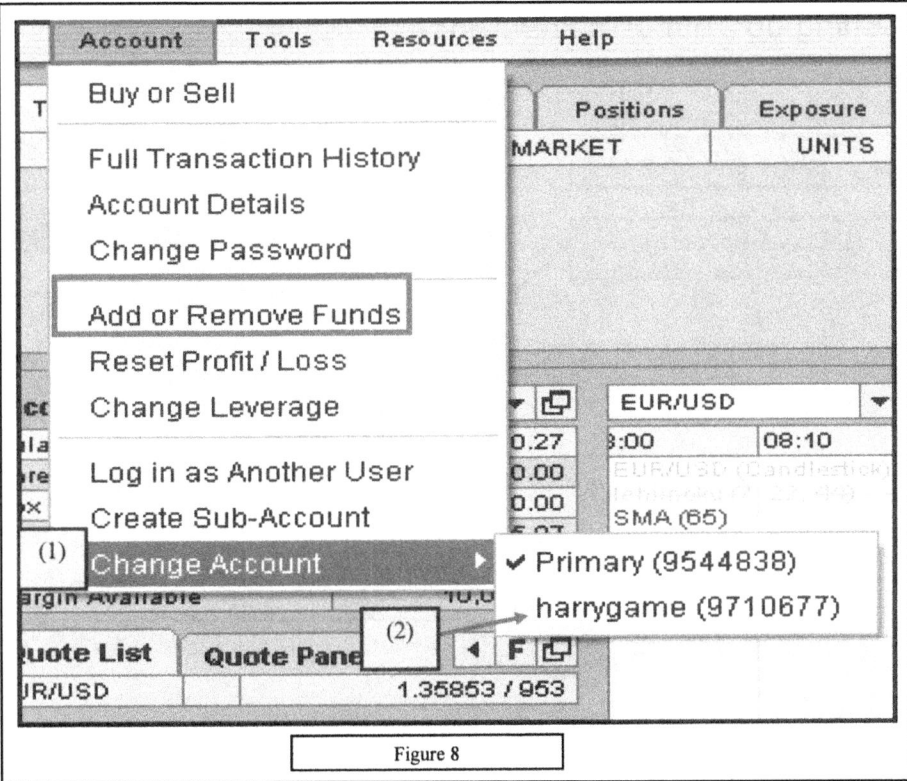

Figure 8

1. Return to the main screen, click, Account, window opens, click on, Change Account.

2. You are in the Primary account, now click on your new, Sub-Account.

3. When you are in your Sub-Account, Deposit $10,000.00, virtual money.

In the Real Money Trading program, "Add or Remove Funds" will say "Transfer Funds".

Same steps but you will transfer real money from your primary account, to your secondary, sub-account.

Each account now starts with, $10,000.00.

The Primary, will BUY Euros, the Secondary will be used to enter, Sell Trades.

## Setting Up Your User Preferences

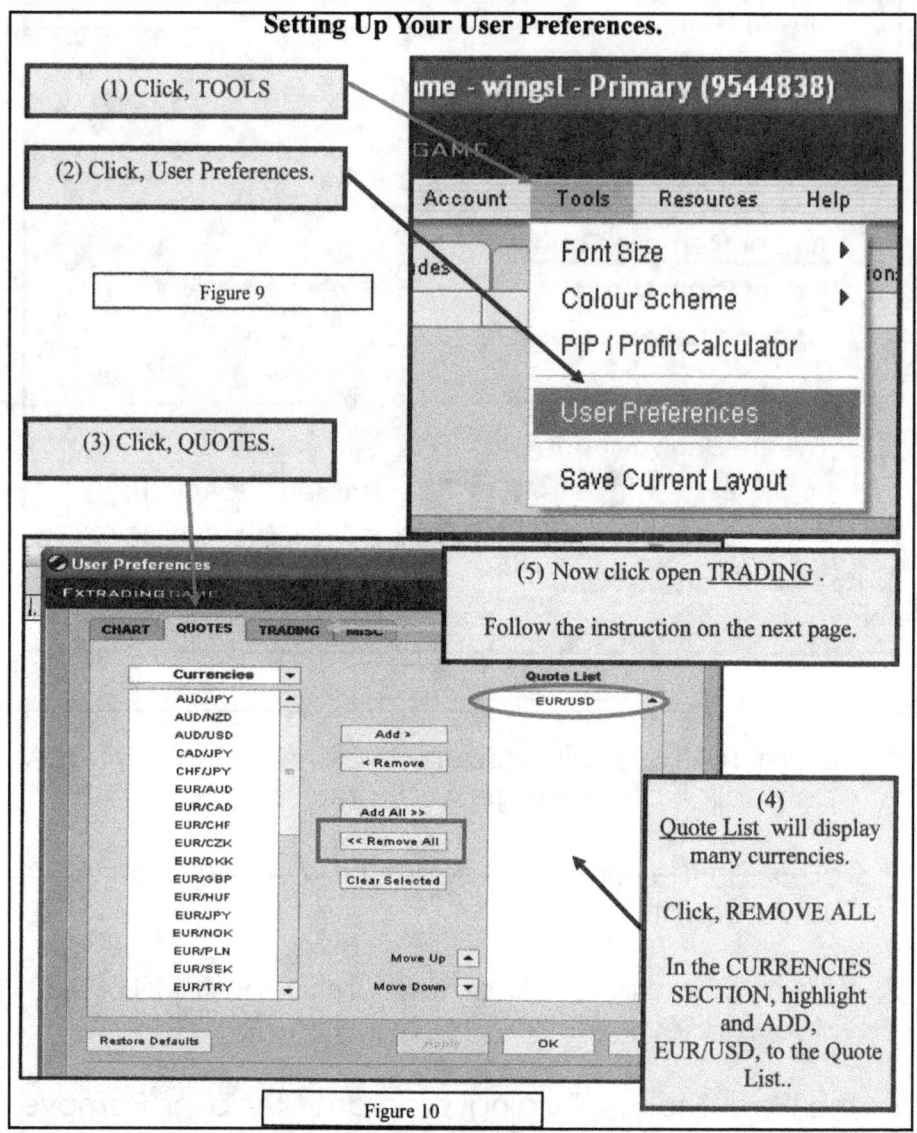

Setting Up Your User Preferences.

(1) Click, TOOLS

(2) Click, User Preferences.

Figure 9

(3) Click, QUOTES.

ame - wingsl - Primary (9544838)

Account    Tools    Resources    Help

Font Size
Colour Scheme
PIP / Profit Calculator
User Preferences
Save Current Layout

(5) Now click open TRADING .

Follow the instruction on the next page.

User Preferences
EXTRADING GAME

CHART    QUOTES    TRADING    MISC.

Currencies
AUD/JPY
AUD/NZD
AUD/USD
CAD/JPY
CHF/JPY
EUR/AUD
EUR/CAD
EUR/CHF
EUR/CZK
EUR/DKK
EUR/GBP
EUR/HUF
EUR/JPY
EUR/NOK
EUR/PLN
EUR/SEK
EUR/TRY

Add >
< Remove

Add All >>
<< Remove All

Clear Selected

Move Up
Move Down

Quote List
EUR/USD

(4)
Quote List  will display many currencies.

Click, REMOVE ALL

In the CURRENCIES SECTION, highlight and ADD, EUR/USD, to the Quote List..

Restore Defaults    Apply    OK

Figure 10

## Trading Preferences

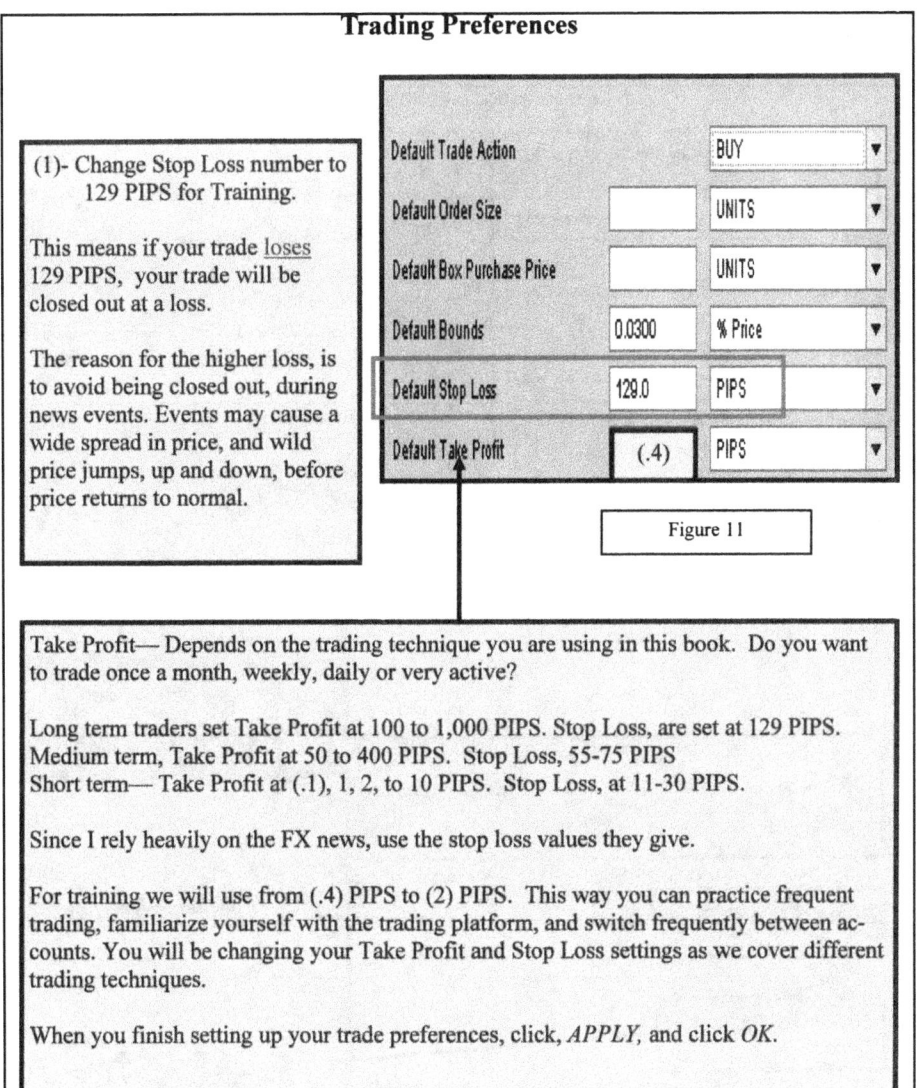

**Trading Preferences**

(1)- Change Stop Loss number to 129 PIPS for Training.

This means if your trade loses 129 PIPS, your trade will be closed out at a loss.

The reason for the higher loss, is to avoid being closed out, during news events. Events may cause a wide spread in price, and wild price jumps, up and down, before price returns to normal.

| | | |
|---|---|---|
| Default Trade Action | | BUY ▼ |
| Default Order Size | | UNITS ▼ |
| Default Box Purchase Price | | UNITS ▼ |
| Default Bounds | 0.0300 | % Price ▼ |
| Default Stop Loss | 129.0 | PIPS ▼ |
| Default Take Profit | (.4) | PIPS ▼ |

Figure 11

Take Profit— Depends on the trading technique you are using in this book. Do you want to trade once a month, weekly, daily or very active?

Long term traders set Take Profit at 100 to 1,000 PIPS. Stop Loss, are set at 129 PIPS.
Medium term, Take Profit at 50 to 400 PIPS. Stop Loss, 55-75 PIPS
Short term— Take Profit at (.1), 1, 2, to 10 PIPS. Stop Loss, at 11-30 PIPS.

Since I rely heavily on the FX news, use the stop loss values they give.

For training we will use from (.4) PIPS to (2) PIPS. This way you can practice frequent trading, familiarize yourself with the trading platform, and switch frequently between accounts. You will be changing your Take Profit and Stop Loss settings as we cover different trading techniques.

When you finish setting up your trade preferences, click, *APPLY,* and click *OK.*

## Main Screen, Account Summary

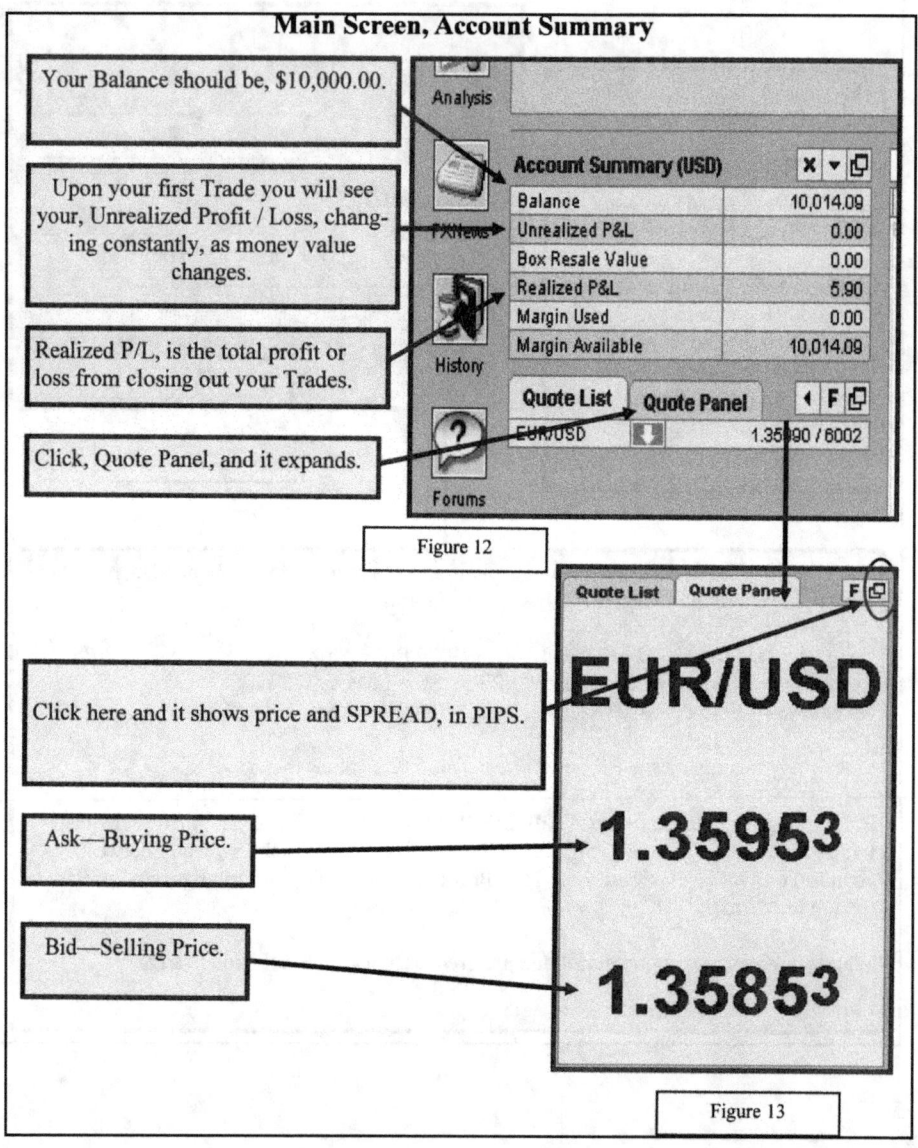

**Main Screen, Account Summary**

Your Balance should be, $10,000.00.

Upon your first Trade you will see your, Unrealized Profit / Loss, changing constantly, as money value changes.

Realized P/L, is the total profit or loss from closing out your Trades.

Click, Quote Panel, and it expands.

Analysis

FXNews

History

Forums

**Account Summary (USD)**

| | |
|---|---|
| Balance | 10,014.09 |
| Unrealized P&L | 0.00 |
| Box Resale Value | 0.00 |
| Realized P&L | 5.90 |
| Margin Used | 0.00 |
| Margin Available | 10,014.09 |

Quote List | Quote Panel

EUR/USD   1.35890 / 6002

Figure 12

Quote List | Quote Panel   F

Click here and it shows price and SPREAD, in PIPS.

Ask—Buying Price.

Bid—Selling Price.

# EUR/USD

# 1.35953

# 1.35853

Figure 13

# PRICE CHART SETUP

The following web site will provide valuable, detailed information on charts, terms, and investments. For book size and simplicity, I cannot cover in detail the different charts. You can study Charts at: http://www.investopedia.com/

One, day chart, *candlestick,* shows how the price moved during a 24 hour period of time. One *candlestick* shows you the low of the day, the high of the day, and if the price closed higher or lower than the previous day. Figure 14, shows white *candlesticks* and dark *candlesticks*. The

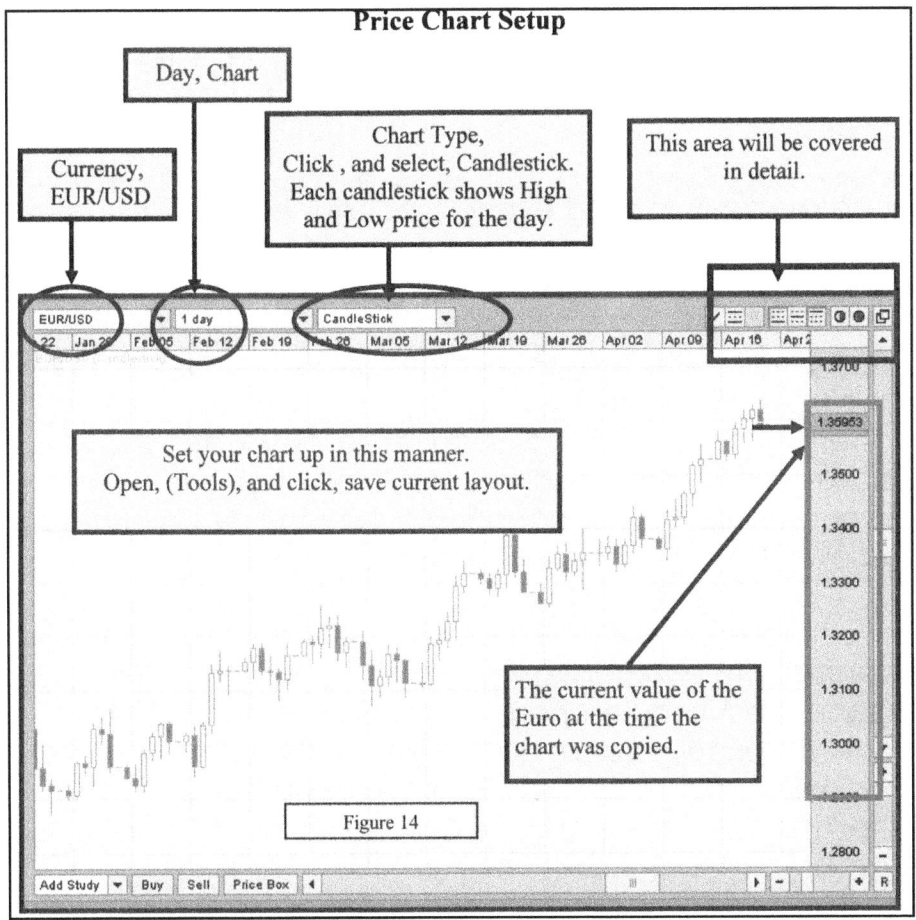

Figure 14

white candle indicates the price closed higher than the start of the day. A black *candlestick* indicates, it closed at a lower price. Several black candles in a row, show a drop in price, while several white candles, reveal a price increase. When you view, figure 14, you will observe many more white candles, than black ones. This indicates a continuing price increase, or an uptrend. We avoid trading against the trend, accept for very active short term trading.

Later, when we view the 3 Hour chart, each candle represents the high and low during a three hour period of time. The 1 Hour, 30 minute, 15 minute, 5 minute, 1 minute, 30 second, 10 second, and 5 second; all follow. Each candlestick will show the price movement, during that period of time.

Each shorter time frame, like a microscope, is revealing what is occurring inside the previous time frames, "candlestick".

Since money is traded every 5 seconds of time, or less, a 5 second chart reveals the price moving up and down constantly.

Every 5 seconds, the price may go up four times then drop three times, and then go up again. Eventually a set pattern of price increases, or decreases will be seen. If a trader looks at the 5 second chart, then changes to the 10 second chart, the 5 second price rise may be confirmed, or viewed, as just a momentary price increase.

Each larger time frame, will add confirmation, to the eventual price increase or decrease. In active trading, we use the 5 minute chart, as the *shortest time frame*, to confirm a price increase or decrease. The section on trend lines, will teach you, that we enter a BUY or SELL order, when the trend line is broken. Like the heavy train, moving down the railroad tracks, we want enough size, (buyers or sellers), and speed of movement, (volume), to be present, before we enter a trade. We call this momentum. When the price increase has enough momentum, it will be harder to stop, and change course. After rising higher, currency will lose momentum, level off, and often drop in price. The price will drop until the market, (buyers), once again buy. When the traders get on board the price train, the price will rise again. When the price is moving sideways, it is best to wait, until everyone starts getting on board, once again.

All the indicators covered in this book, will automatically adjust to the sensitivity of each shorter time frame. The indicators will tell you what is taking place within that specific time frame. Starting with the shortest time frame, and viewing the larger time frames, will provide a better perspective on price direction.

## Adding Information to the Price Chart

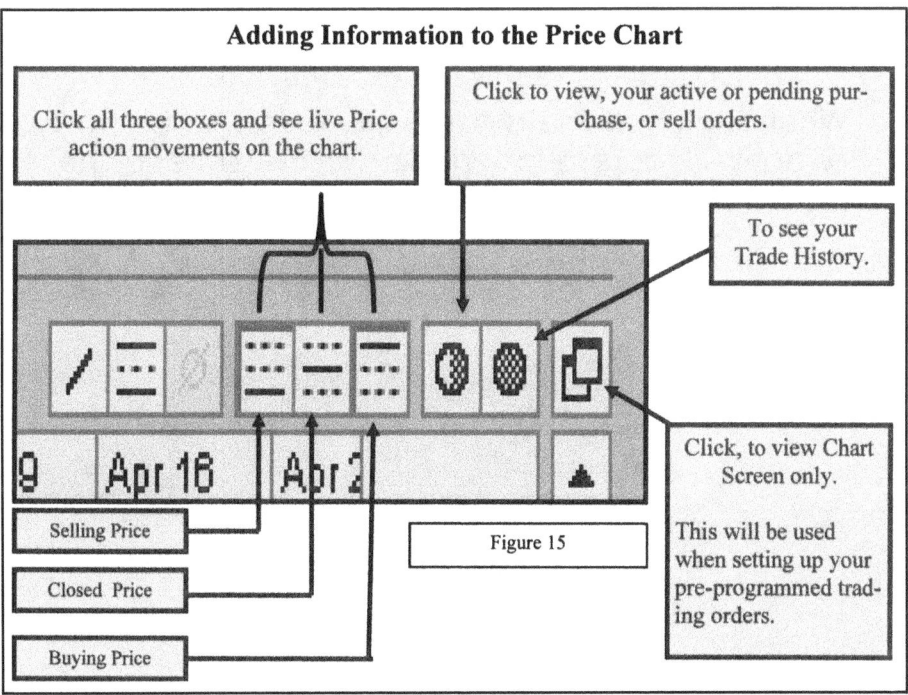

Adding Information to the Price Chart

Click all three boxes and see live Price action movements on the chart.

Click to view, your active or pending purchase, or sell orders.

To see your Trade History.

Click, to view Chart Screen only.

This will be used when setting up your pre-programmed trading orders.

Selling Price

Closed Price

Buying Price

Figure 15

On your computer, look at the top of the Price Chart Screen.

Click, Day view, then the 3 hour view, 1 hour, 5 minutes, 1 minute, 30 second, and 10 second view. Each Price Chart reveals a candle stick price range, indicating the high or low price for that period of time. Each chart will show the currency either rising or falling in value.

On the next page we will draw lines across the top of the price line, the mountain peaks, and below, the valleys. We call these lines, trend lines. Trend lines will point in a direction, either up, down, or sideways. This reveals the currency's trend, to increase or decrease in value.

The line, on top of the peaks, will be called, resistance, to further price increase.

The line, drawn below, will be referred to as, support, preventing further price decline.

When the price line moves up through, resistance or down through support, we will call a trend line breakout.

# TRADING TREND LINES

As simple, as it may seem, the ability to draw trend lines will be used repeatedly, to determine entry, and exit points, for a trade. Trend lines will be used in combination with other indicators to provide confirmation, on timing a trade. Become familiar drawing trend lines in the FX game platform.

Figure 16, zooms in on to the upper right hand corner of the chart screen.

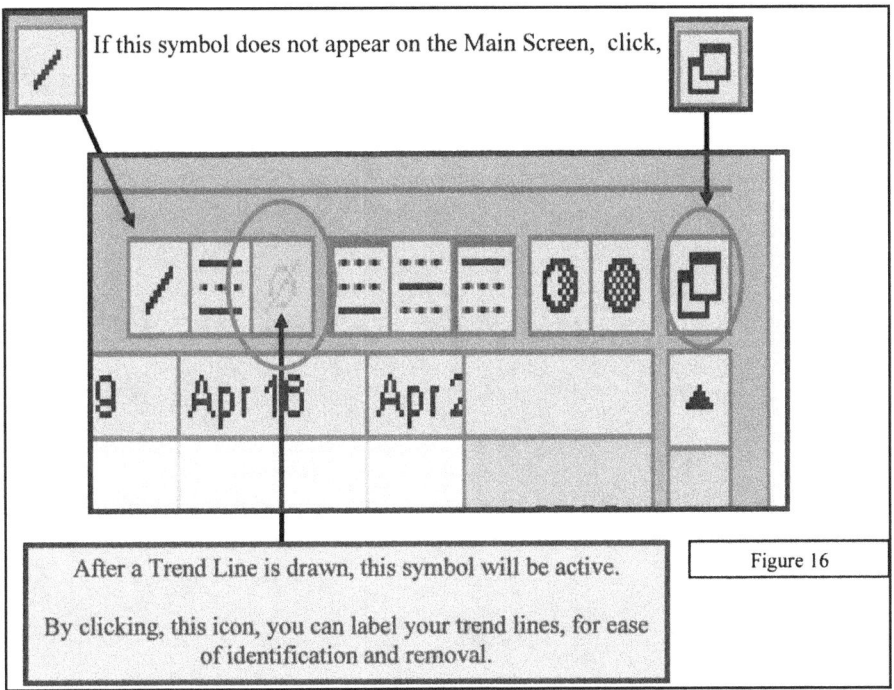

If this symbol does not appear on the Main Screen, click,

After a Trend Line is drawn, this symbol will be active.

By clicking, this icon, you can label your trend lines, for ease of identification and removal.

Figure 16

# DRAWING TREND LINES

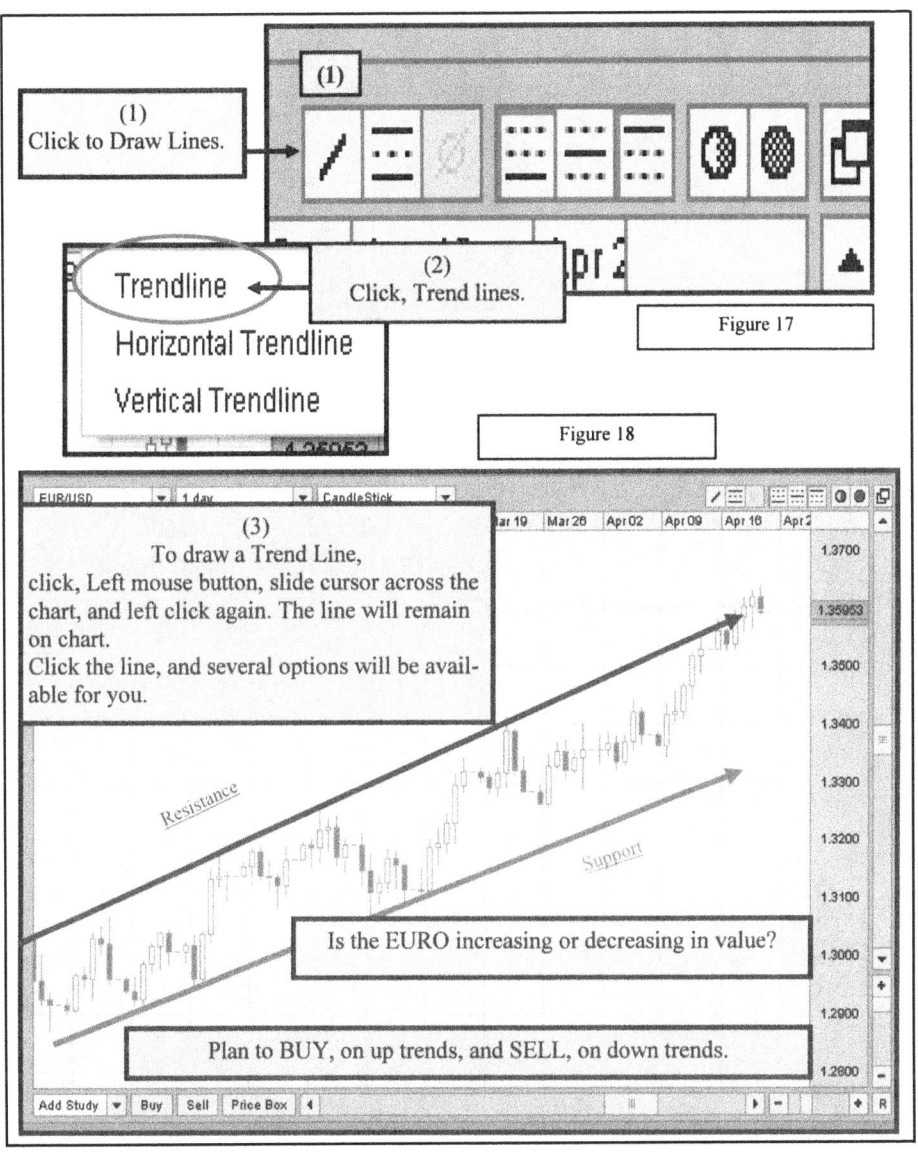

(1)

(1) Click to Draw Lines.

(2) Click, Trend lines.

Trendline

Horizontal Trendline

Vertical Trendline

Figure 17

Figure 18

(3)
To draw a Trend Line,
click, Left mouse button, slide cursor across the
chart, and left click again. The line will remain
on chart.
Click the line, and several options will be available for you.

Resistance

Support

Is the EURO increasing or decreasing in value?

Plan to BUY, on up trends, and SELL, on down trends.

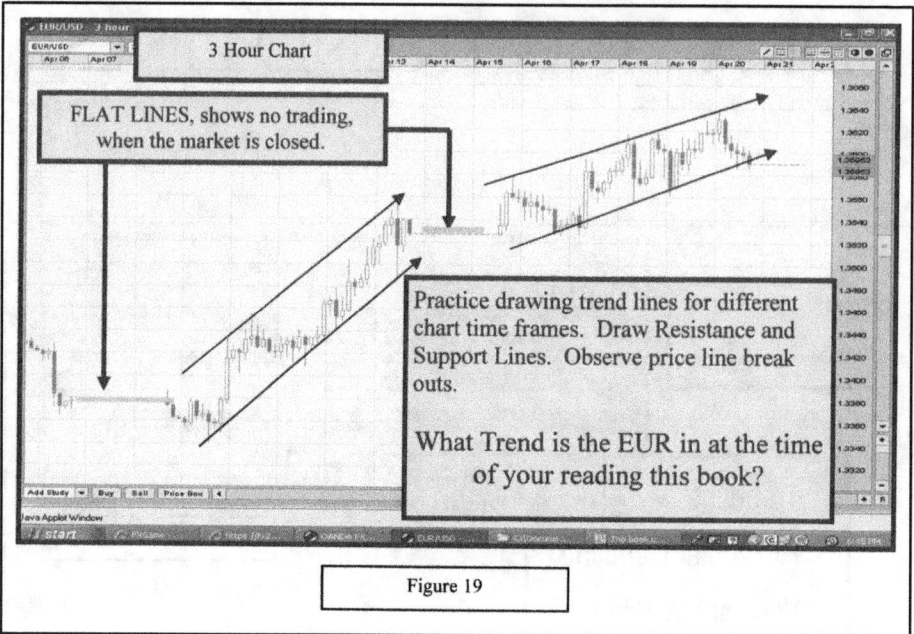

FLAT LINES, shows no trading, when the market is closed.

3 Hour Chart

Practice drawing trend lines for different chart time frames. Draw Resistance and Support Lines. Observe price line break outs.

What Trend is the EUR in at the time of your reading this book?

Figure 19

The 3 Hour Chart—Shows the currency trend, which is up. Inside the channel it moves up, down or sideways. These are opportunities for either Buying or Selling the EURO.

If you see a Sideways Pattern—the market is uncertain about the direction. This is a difficult trade. Wait and read the FX news, for hints on future price direction.

Enter large orders with the trend, (10,000 units), and smaller orders against it, (1000 units). Practice drawing trend lines for different chart time frames. Draw Resistance and Support Lines. Observe price line break outs.

# TREND LINE BREAKOUTS

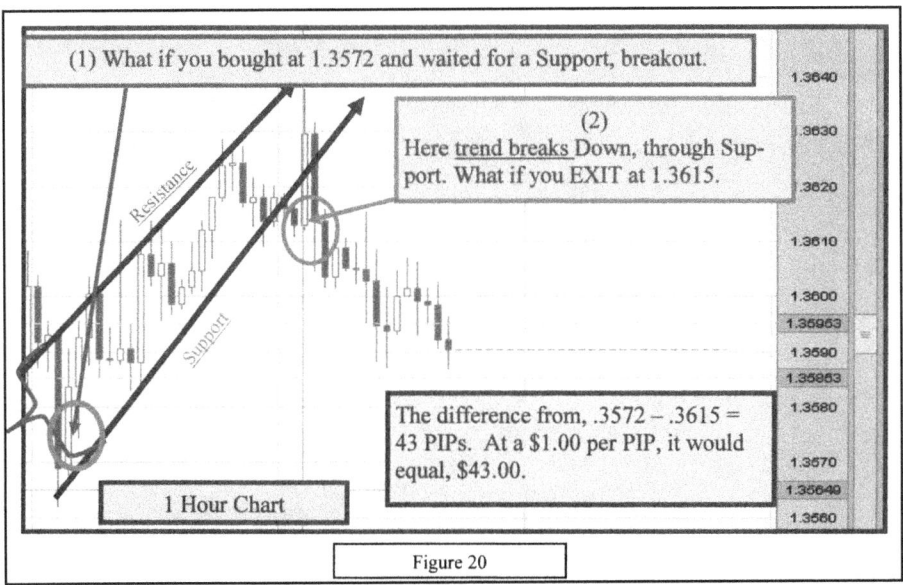

(1) What if you bought at 1.3572 and waited for a Support, breakout.

(2)
Here trend breaks Down, through Support. What if you EXIT at 1.3615.

The difference from, .3572 – .3615 = 43 PIPs. At a $1.00 per PIP, it would equal, $43.00.

1 Hour Chart

1.3640
.3630
.3620
1.3610
1.3600
1.35953
1.3590
1.35853
1.3580
1.3570
1.35649
1.3560

Figure 20

Using the Hour Chart—if, we had entered, a "Buy" Trade, when bouncing off Support, and had exited, "Sold", when breaking down through the support line, we would have achieved a profit.

Trend lines—will be one of several tools used to determine a BUY or SELL signal.

The Day Chart will be our guide, for long term trend indications. If the trend is UP, (Bullish), we will purchase more units, entering a Buy order, and purchase a smaller number of units, when entering a Sell order.

If the trend starts DOWN, (Bearish), we will purchase larger amounts entering a Sell order, and purchase fewer units, when entering a BUY trade. Make your bigger, unit purchases, with the Trend.

The 15 minute, 5 minute, 1 minute, and 30 second charts, will be used for active trading.

# DRAWING TREND LINES TO DETERMINE CHART PATTERNS

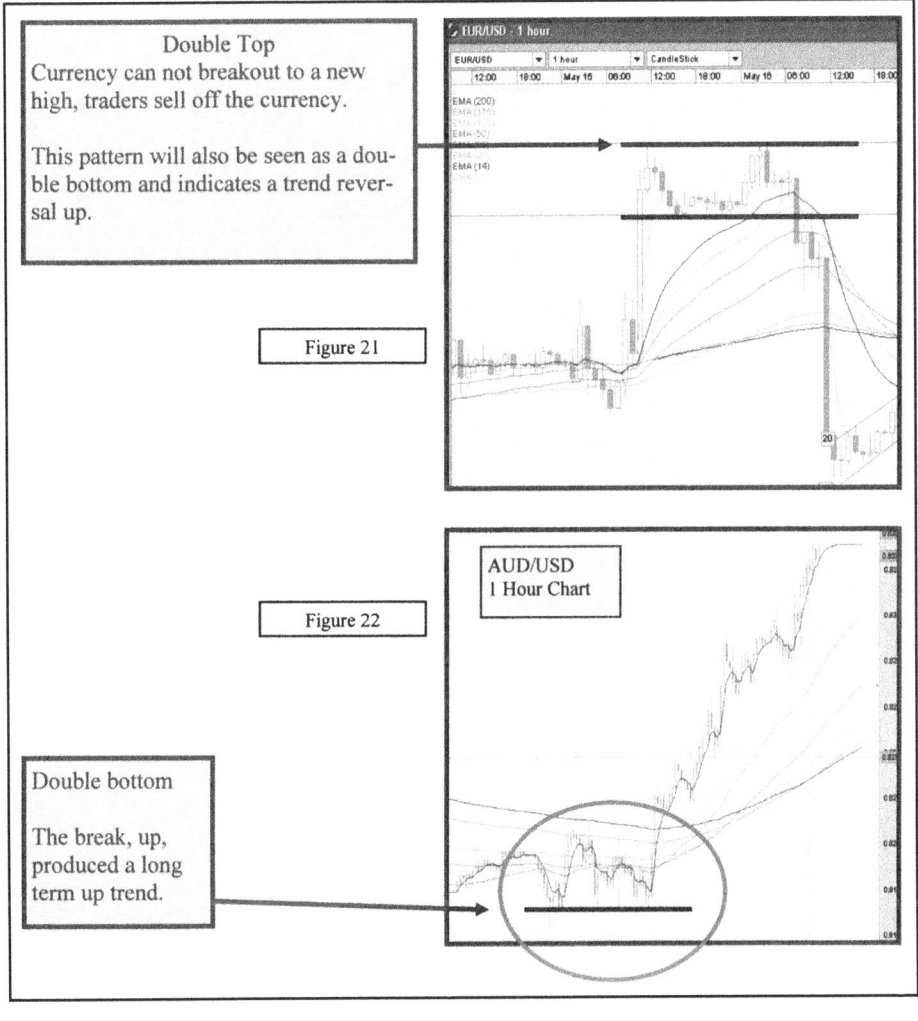

**Double Top**
Currency can not breakout to a new high, traders sell off the currency.

This pattern will also be seen as a double bottom and indicates a trend reversal up.

Figure 21

Figure 22

AUD/USD
1 Hour Chart

Double bottom

The break, up, produced a long term up trend.

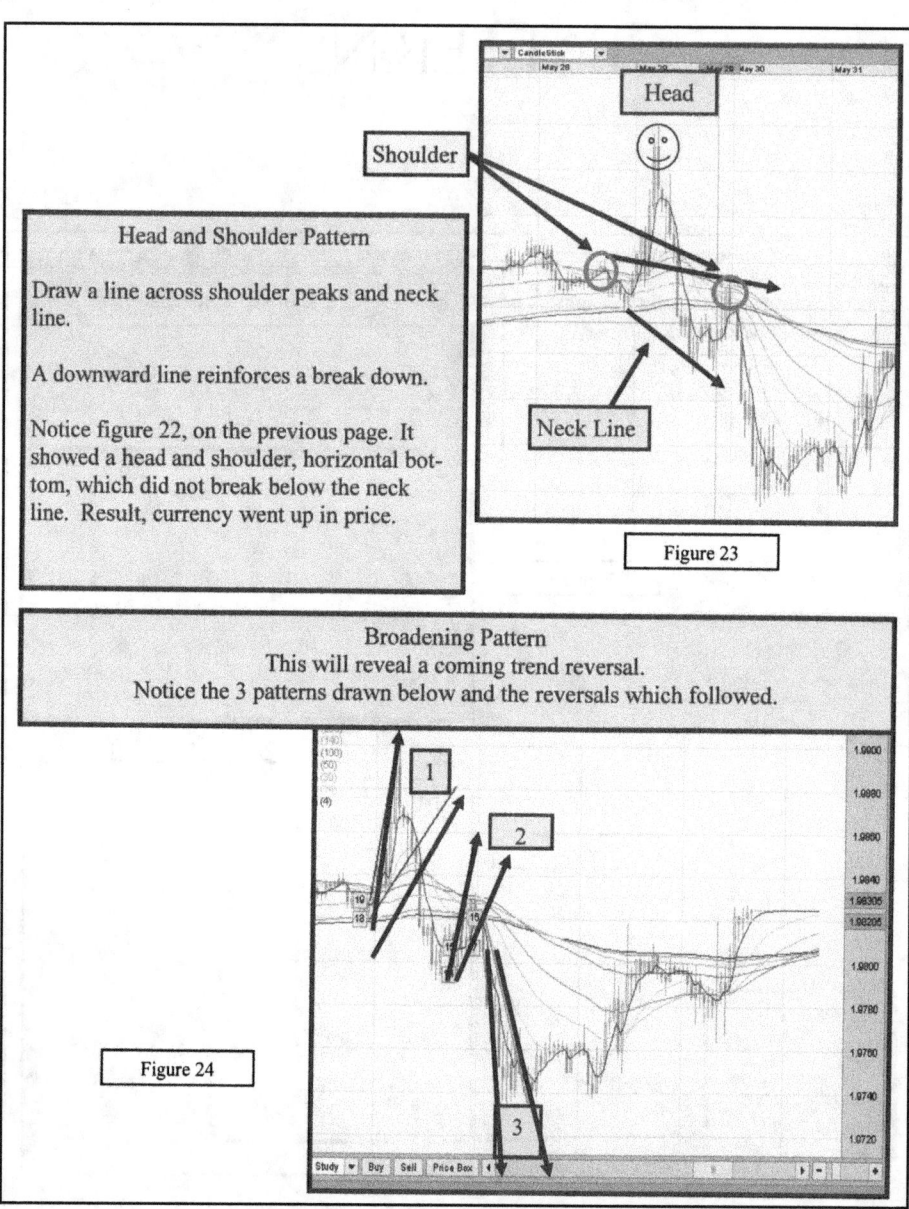

**Head and Shoulder Pattern**

Draw a line across shoulder peaks and neck line.

A downward line reinforces a break down.

Notice figure 22, on the previous page. It showed a head and shoulder, horizontal bottom, which did not break below the neck line. Result, currency went up in price.

Head

Shoulder

Neck Line

Figure 23

**Broadening Pattern**
This will reveal a coming trend reversal.
Notice the 3 patterns drawn below and the reversals which followed.

Figure 24

# TRADING TRIANGLES

There are 3 types of Triangles — Ascending, Descending and Symmetrical.

Chart books teach that ascending triangles mean an upward price increase, descending triangles, a downward price break, and symmetrical triangles, can go either way. I have looked at several Forex charts and the only thing that triangles have shown me, a break is certain, and the direction is unknown. I will present several triangle patterns and let you decide. You can view price charts, draw triangles, and make your own mind up.

Trade Technique
The next page will display a 15 minute Price Chart. Had you placed an entry order, to Buy, 6 PIPs, above the triangle, and enter a Sell order, (in your sub-account), 6 PIPs, below, the triangle, one of the orders would have triggered.

If the EXIT, Take Profit, was 4 PIPs, you would have made money each time.

In a triangle pattern, the high and low price range narrows, price pressure builds, and a sharp increase or decrease in price results. Practice using the two accounts. Enter a Buy order in one account, 6 PIPs above the triangle, and a sell order in the other account, 6 PIPs below the triangle. Pre-program your Take Profit, at 4PIPs. Example, line #15 and #14, shows drawn trend line, at top and bottom. For a BUY order, add 6 PIPs to .3458 which equals, .3464. A BUY order would be entered at 1.3464 and a take profit, exit at, (+4PIPs), or 1.3468. Using the price of, 1.3456, a SELL order would be entered at, (−6PIPs), 1.3450. The exit, (−4 PIPs), take profit would be set at 1.3446.

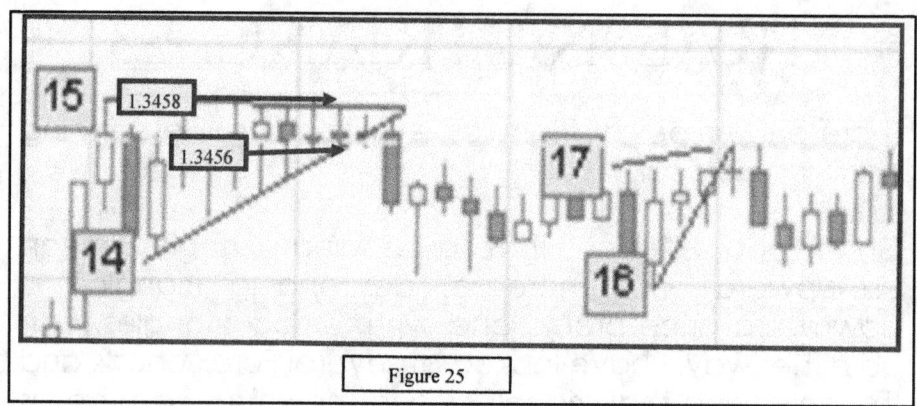

Figure 25

Using the 15 minute Price Chart, the trading technique covered on the previous page, a trader would have made money, on every triangle shown below. If you can draw a line, do some simple math, you could obtain the same results.

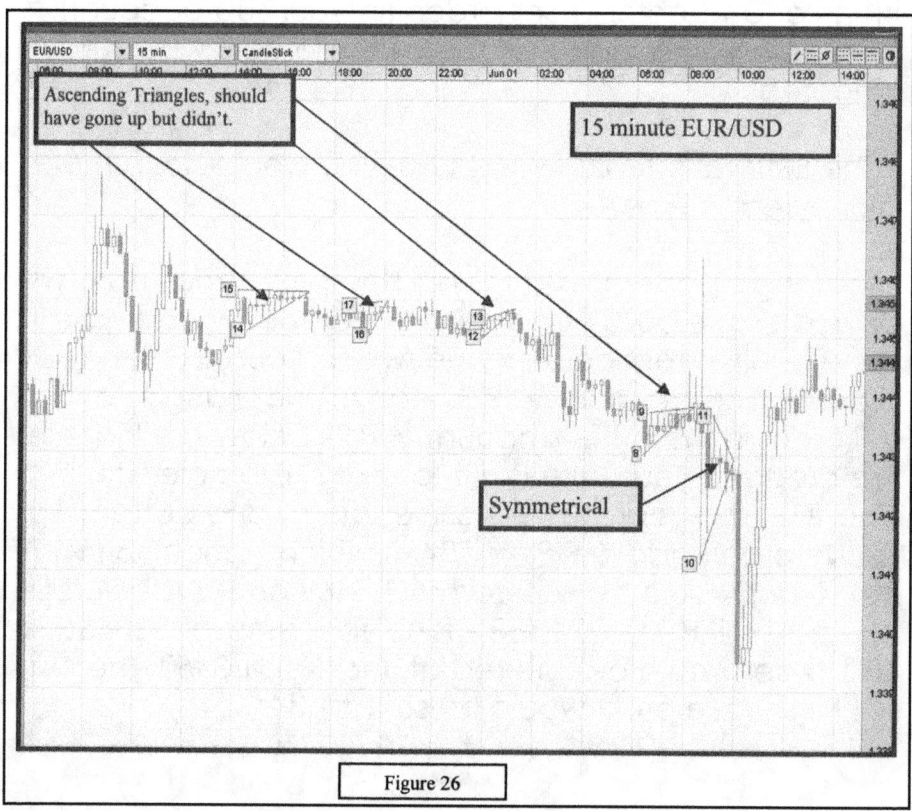

Figure 26

## Trading Trend Line Breakouts

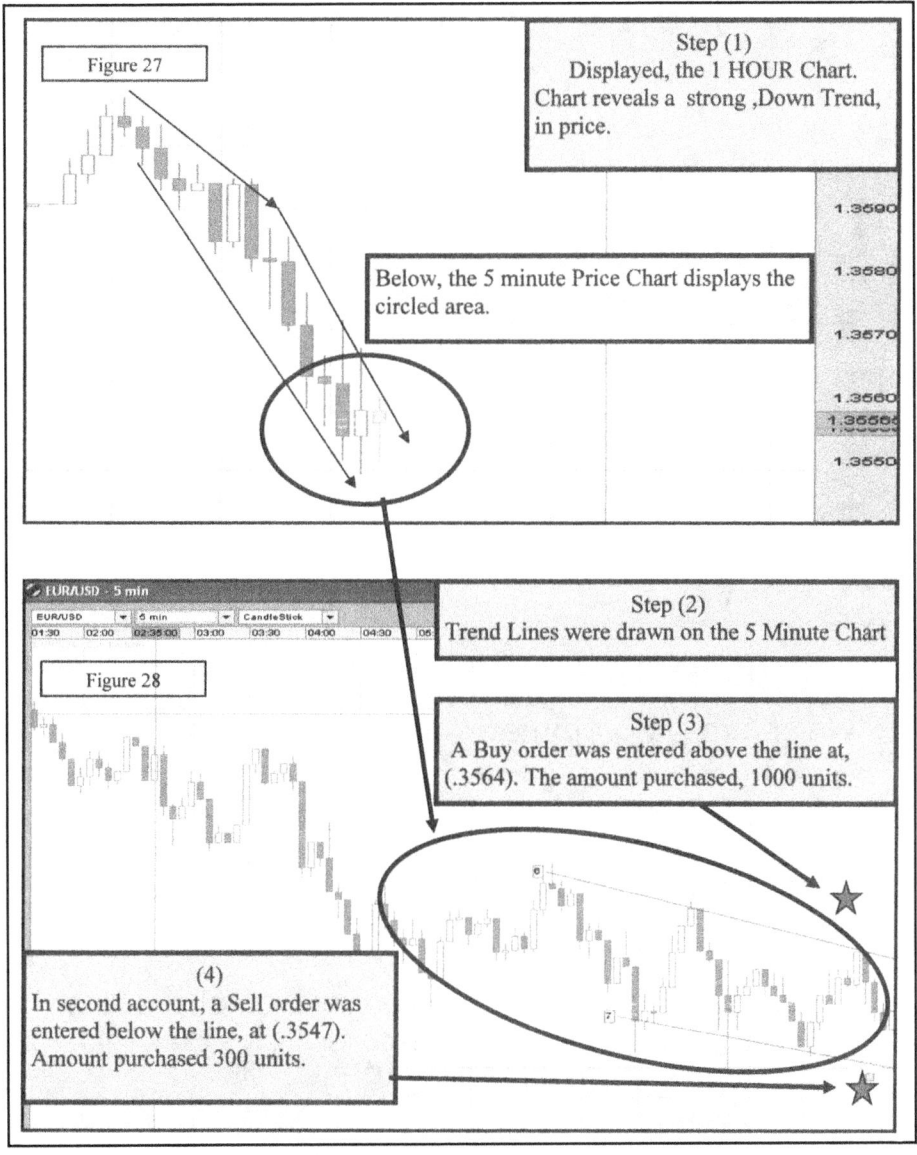

Figure 27

**Step (1)**
Displayed, the 1 HOUR Chart.
Chart reveals a strong ,Down Trend,
in price.

Below, the 5 minute Price Chart displays the
circled area.

1.3590
1.3580
1.3570
1.3560
1.35565
1.3550

EUR/USD - 5 min

EUR/USD | 5 min | CandleStick
01:30 | 02:00 | 02:35:00 | 03:00 | 03:30 | 04:00 | 04:30 | 05

**Step (2)**
Trend Lines were drawn on the 5 Minute Chart

Figure 28

**Step (3)**
A Buy order was entered above the line at,
(.3564). The amount purchased, 1000 units.

**(4)**
In second account, a Sell order was
entered below the line, at (.3547).
Amount purchased 300 units.

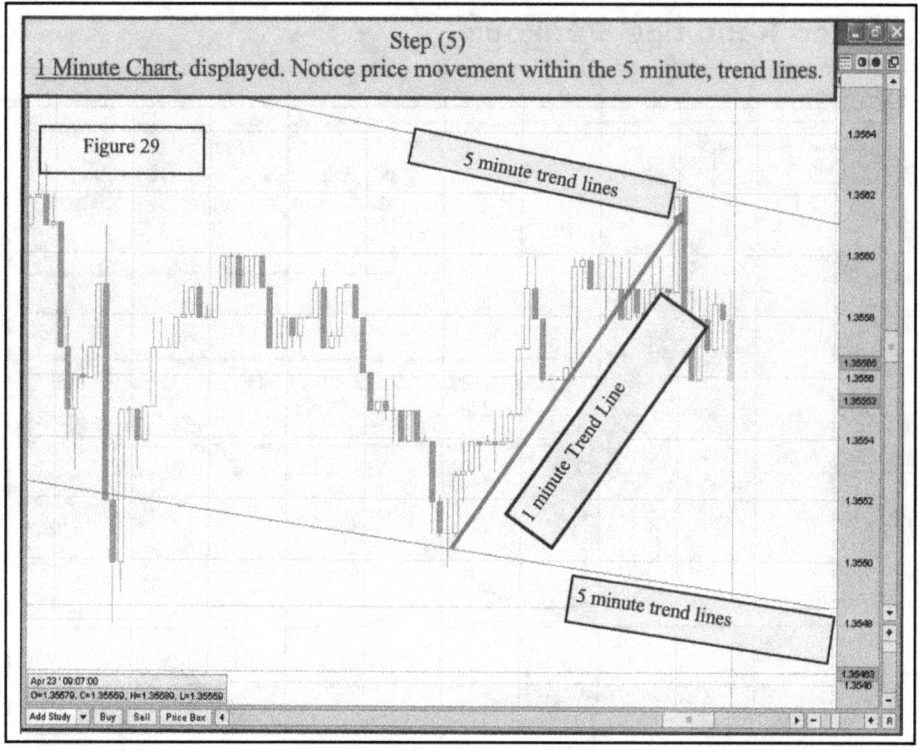

**Step (5)**
__1 Minute Chart__, displayed. Notice price movement within the 5 minute, trend lines.

Figure 29

5 minute trend lines

1 minute Trend Line

5 minute trend lines

Apr 23 ' 09:07:00
O=1.35579, C=1.35559, H=1.35589, L=1.35559

Add Study ▼ | Buy | Sell | Price Box | ◄

Which pre-programmed Trade order was correct?

We used, one, of two accounts. A 300 Unit, pre-programmed Sell order at, (.3547), was placed. The trade Exit point, (Take Profit), was placed at 3 PIPs, (.3544).

In the Buy account, 1000 units were purchased, a BUY order, at (.3564), was entered. The Exit, Take Profit, was placed at 3 PIPs, (.3567).

Both of these pre-programmed, _pending_ Orders were placed, __above and below__ the __5 minute__, "Trend Line", in order to play both sides of the trade.

In short term trading use the 5 minute price chart, to draw your trend lines. Then wait for a clean break above the resistance or support line.

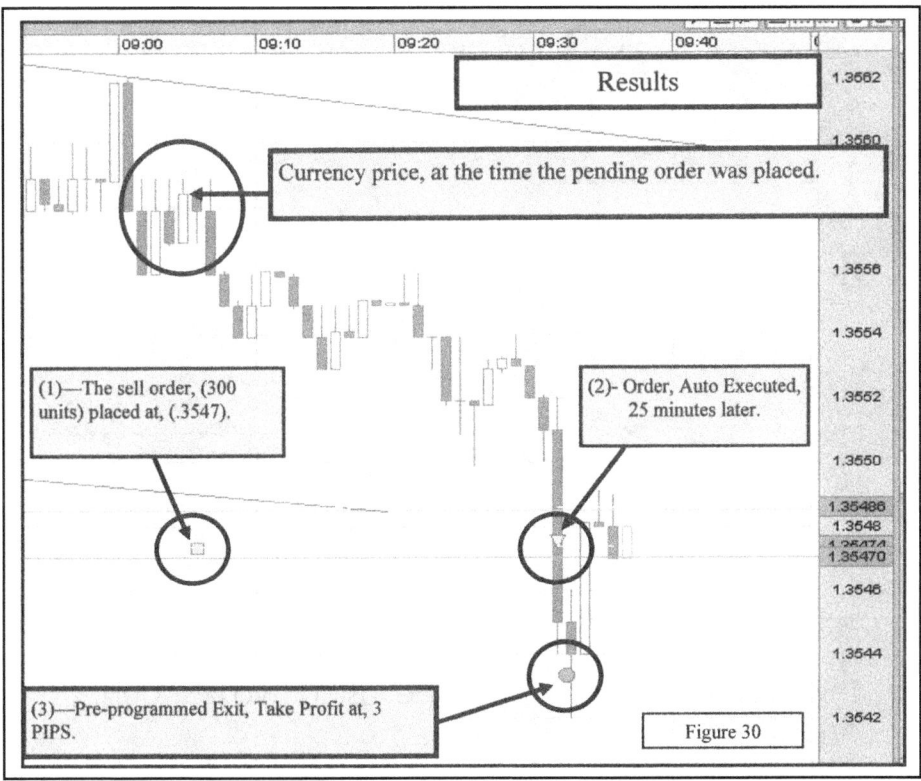

Results

Currency price, at the time the pending order was placed.

(1)—The sell order, (300 units) placed at, (.3547).

(2)- Order, Auto Executed, 25 minutes later.

(3)—Pre-programmed Exit, Take Profit at, 3 PIPS.

Figure 30

When the BUY and SELL orders were placed, we had no idea if the, 5 minute Trend Line would be broken, to the Downside, or to the UP side, of the Channel.

It broke down, the order was executed automatically, and closed out automatically, at a profit.

Since the major Day Chart Trend was UP, the trade was against the trend, and therefore smaller unit amounts were purchased.

As you will see on the following page, the pending BUY order, was still in place.

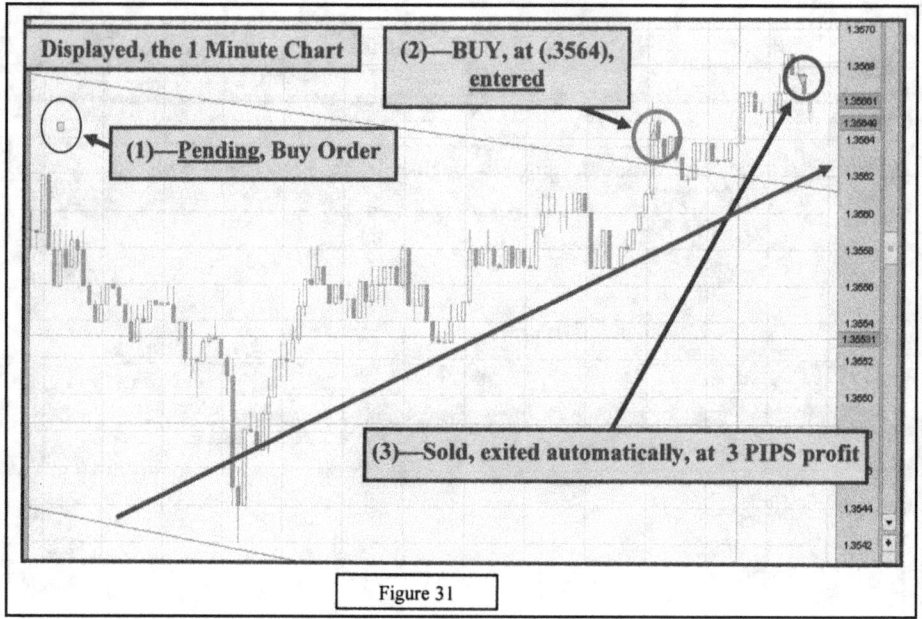

Figure 31

This showed a short term trade, using two accounts, and 5 minute price chart.

If only one account was used, both sides of the trade would not have been possible.

Six PIPs, total profit resulted from the two accounts, in 30 minutes of time.

Six PIPs can be worth 6 cents, for 100 units, 60 cents, for a 1,000 units, $6.00 for 10,000 units, $60.00 for 100,000 units, or $600.00 for 600,000 units. The profit is determined by the number of units purchased.

My goal is to train you to safely earn pennies, which can turn to dimes, which grows into dollars.

We live in amazing and exciting times. From the comfort of your home or from a mobile wireless laptop, you can be trading the world currencies.

If you were a passenger on a long highway trip, had wireless internet connection, you could turn idle road trip hours, into dollars, with the click of a mouse.

This section covered <u>one simple subject</u>—*Trend Lines and Chart Patterns.*

You should practice trading, using the simple, Trend Line technique.

## Trade Technique

- Draw the top and bottom Trend Lines for the DAY Price Chart. This will tell you the long term trend.
- What is the major Day Chart trend for the EUR/USD?
- View the 5 min and 1 min Chart for active trading, and follow the steps listed below.
- Draw the resistance and support, trend lines, on the 5 minute chart.
- In the game account, buy more units <u>*with the trend*</u>, (10,000) and fewer units, (1000) against the major trend. When the price line <u>*nears*</u> a support or resistance line, make a note where a possible trading, entry point would be, on the 5 minute chart.
- Using the 5 minute chart, place an entry order, <u>3 PIPs</u>, above, the resistance line, (BUY), and below, the support line, (SELL), in each ,of the two accounts. *We are looking to Enter the Trade, when the trend line is broken.*
- Your exit point will be 2 PIPs profit. You would add the number to a BUY order, and subtract it from your Sell order.
- Money management—Go to your account tab, open user preference, open trading, and set up the following default settings. Take Profit, 2 PIPs, Stop Loss 25 PIPs. Experiment with 10 and 5 PIPs Stop Loss. Two PIPs gain and two PIPs stop loss places you in a 50% chance of winning on the trade. You may get stopped out often, but in the end you will win. Keep a record and

compare different scenarios. When you first enter your order, just click the Take Profit and Stop Loss box. The numbers will be automatically filled in for you. If you are watching your trade, do not enter a stop loss. Exit if the trade loses too many PIPs. The game account is the place to learn and discover.

- Try larger purchases, 100,000 units, in the game platform, and notice the price paid and the resulting gain or loss.

# HOW TO PLACE AN ORDER

Go to the Main Screen, follow the steps shown in figure 32, either click, check or enter numbers. Be careful to enter price numbers correctly.

Hit submit and your order is pending.

On the upper right corner of the Chart, click the active order icon, and see it on the chart screen.

This is the BUY account. Go to the SELL account, and repeat the order entry steps. This time click—SELL.

See which account closes out first. You can adjust your pending order, right on the screen. Click the order icon, (a small box symbol), click modify, and move the mouse cursor to the new price location. Click the left mouse button, and the small price box icon, repositions.

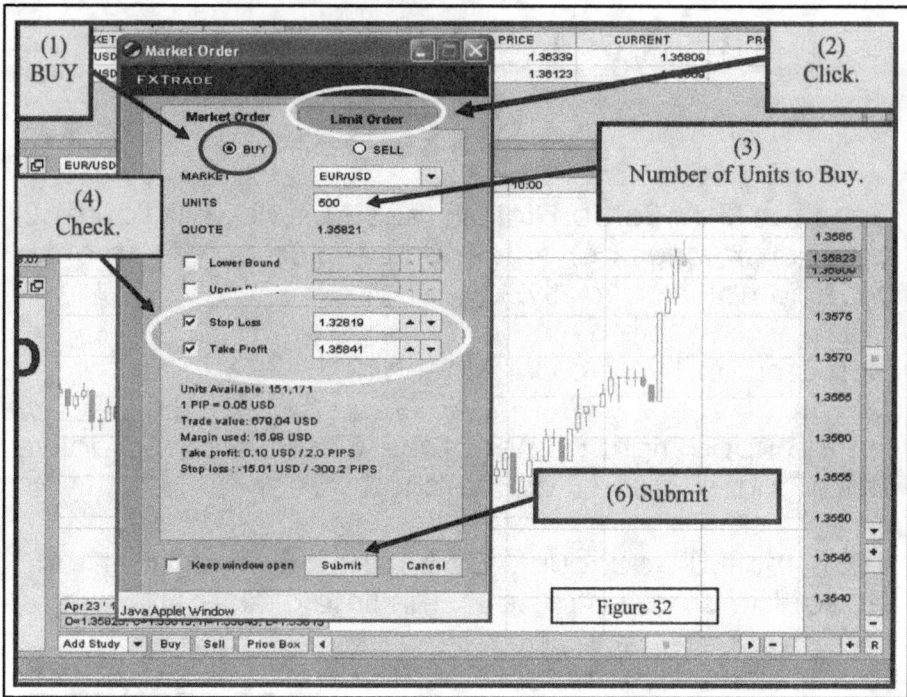

Figure 32

You can also cancel or change the profit/loss line in the same manner. Just place the cursor on the green or red line, left click, and the box opens. Select a choice, move the cursor up or down the chart. When you left click, your mouse again, the line moves to new location.

# NEWS THAT CAN MAKE YOU MONEY!

Oanda has <u>powerful news sources,</u> available at no cost. It is very important that you open and read the news sources. Open the Analysis icon, and the FX News. Terms that you do not understand can be defined at, investopedia.com., by typing the term in the <u>keyword box</u>, and the definition will appear. On page 88, of this book I have additional news terms defined. The following samples illustrate some of the valuable news information.

<u>4 Cast news service</u>, an excellent news service which provides trading advice and financial reports to major banks and corporations. Their web site is, <u>http://www.4castweb.com/</u>

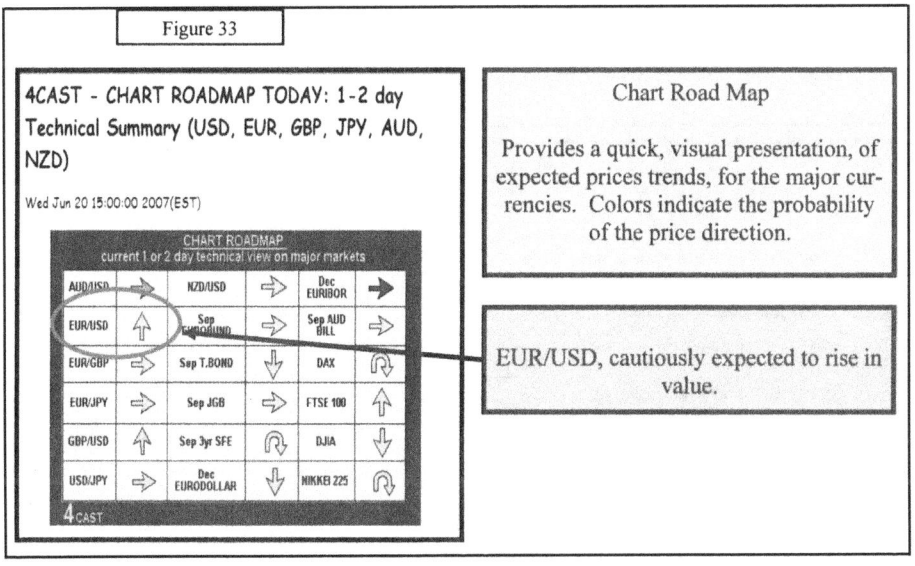

Figure 33

| 4CAST - CHART ROADMAP TODAY: 1-2 day Technical Summary (USD, EUR, GBP, JPY, AUD, NZD) | Chart Road Map |
| --- | --- |
| Wed Jun 20 15:00:00 2007(EST) | Provides a quick, visual presentation, of expected prices trends, for the major currencies. Colors indicate the probability of the price direction. |

EUR/USD, cautiously expected to rise in value.

Another 4Cast news item is, <u>FX Chart EUR/USD</u>. Figure 34, is a sample of what you would see.

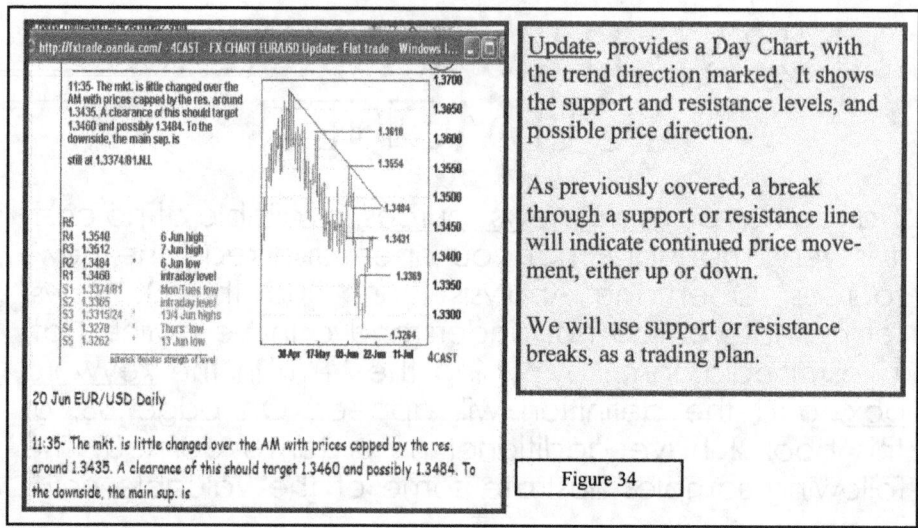

Figure 34

Another trading guide is, <u>Thompson Financial News</u>, figure 35. Click open, FX NEWS. Open Trading Briefs, and click open, EUR/USD. A sample is shown below, (1) Current price. (2) Enter a Sell Order, if price fails to increase, past 1.3705. (3) Enter a Sell Order, if price goes down, past 1.3630. (4) Exit, from your Sell position, if price bounces up. (5) Exit, take profit. Should the price fall further, enter another Sell order, again.

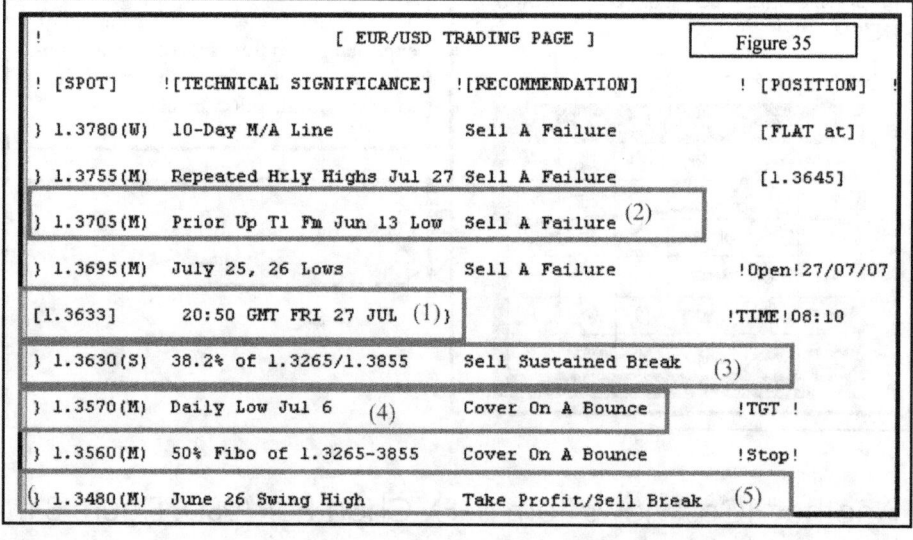

Figure 35

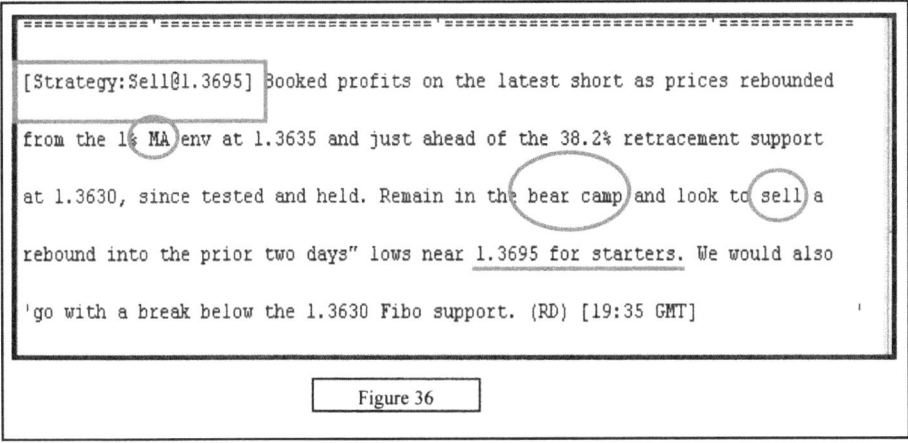

Figure 36

What figure 36 is reporting—Place a Sell Order, below 1.3695. MA, stands for, moving average line, which we will cover.

Bear camp, the price will fall. If the price moves up, be ready to enter a, Sell Order.

Enter a Sell order, if prices move down from 1.3695.

You are receiving valuable information from the experts. While you are learning, do what the news says, and do not trade against it.

**Trading the NEWS!**

Using 4Cast News, update, the following pages will display, six days of visual news presentations.

We will focus our attention to the support and resistance levels noted for, S-1 and R-1 . We will use these values to determine our BUY and SELL entry points.

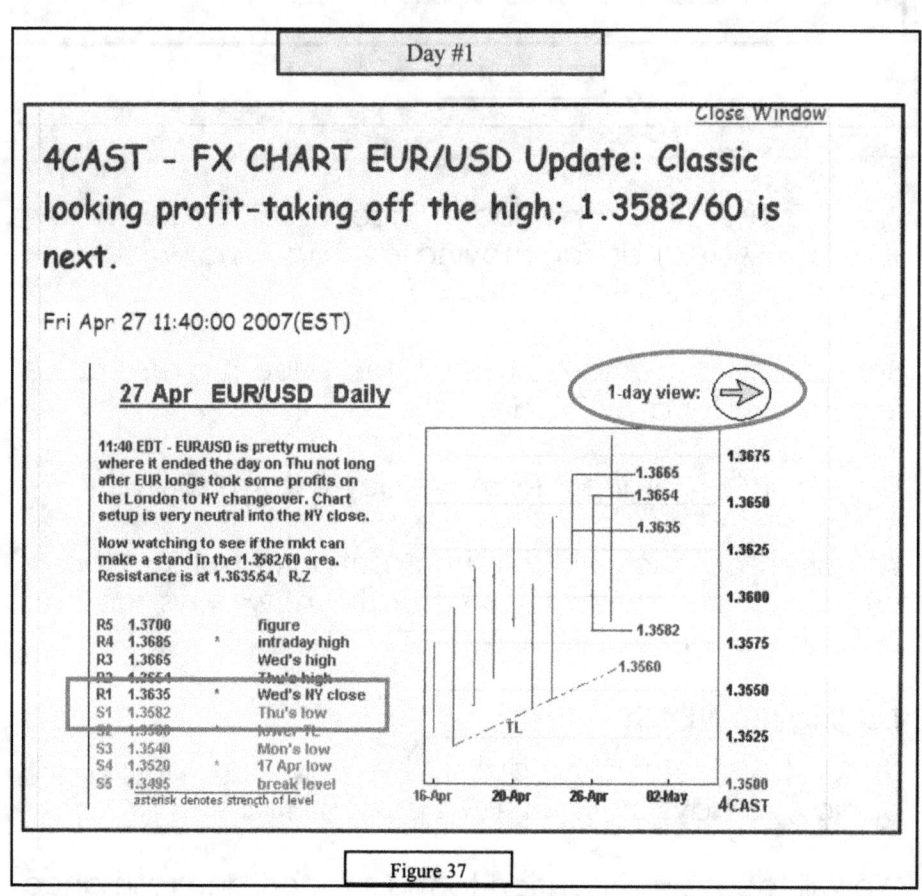

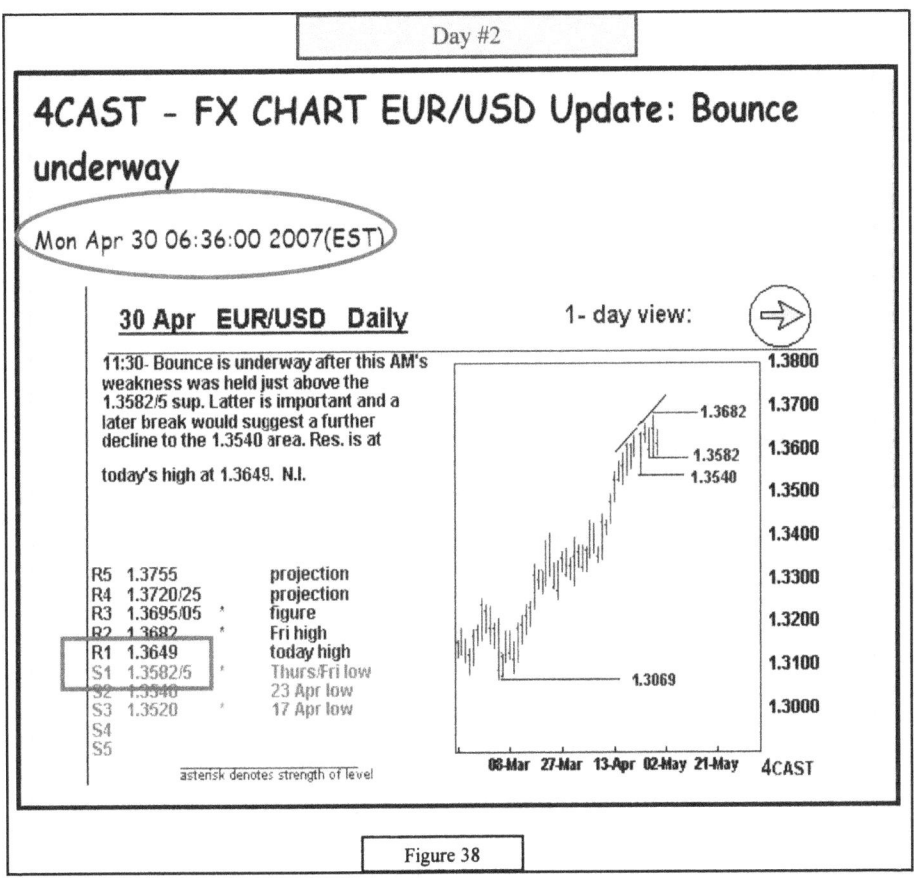

Figure 38

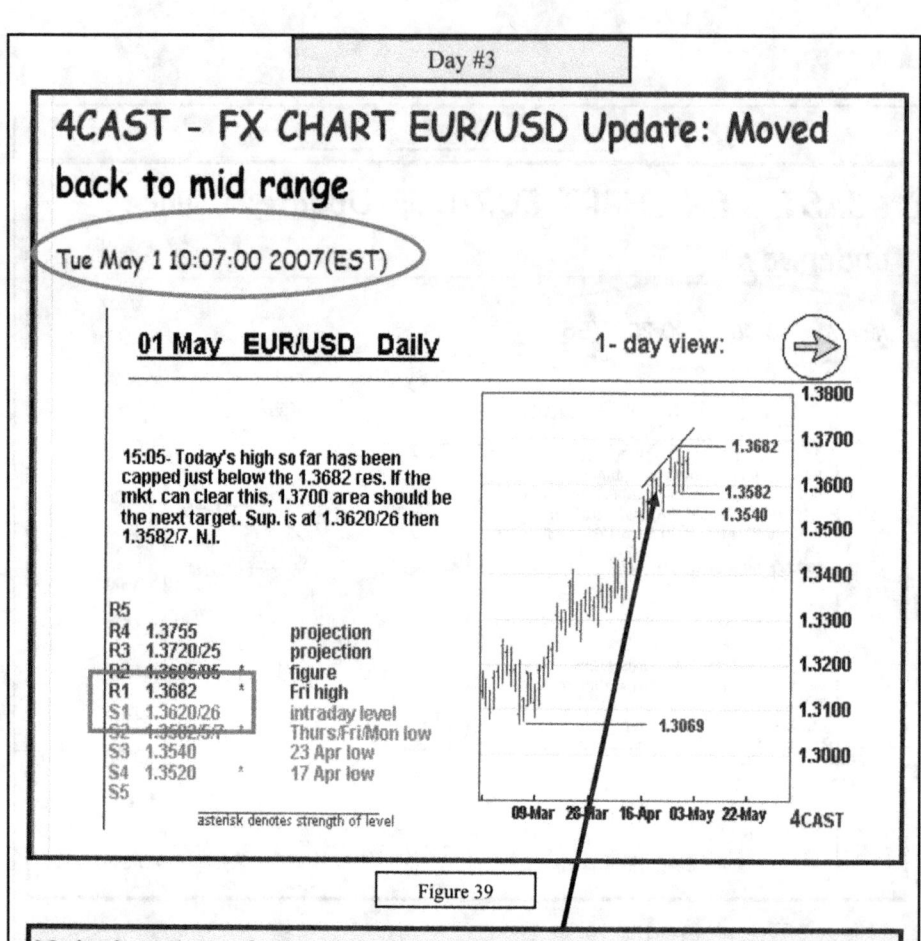

| Day #3 |
| --- |

## 4CAST - FX CHART EUR/USD Update: Moved back to mid range

Tue May 1 10:07:00 2007(EST)

**01 May  EUR/USD  Daily**          1- day view:

15:05- Today's high so far has been capped just below the 1.3682 res. If the mkt. can clear this, 1.3700 area should be the next target. Sup. is at 1.3620/26 then 1.3582/7. N.I.

| | | |
| --- | --- | --- |
| R5 | | |
| R4 | 1.3755 | projection |
| R3 | 1.3720/25 | projection |
| R2 | 1.3605/85 | figure |
| R1 | 1.3682 * | Fri high |
| S1 | 1.3620/26 | intraday level |
| S2 | 1.3582/57 | Thurs/Fri/Mon low |
| S3 | 1.3540 | 23 Apr low |
| S4 | 1.3520 * | 17 Apr low |
| S5 | | |

asterisk denotes strength of level

1.3800
1.3700
1.3682
1.3600
1.3582
1.3540
1.3500
1.3400
1.3300
1.3200
1.3100
1.3069
1.3000

09-Mar  28-Mar  16-Apr  03-May  22-May    4CAST

| Figure 39 |
| --- |

Notice how the professional Traders use Trend Lines, (TL), to determine resistance to price increases.

News reports come out every 3 hours, or more frequently, if needed, to keep you informed.

Day #4

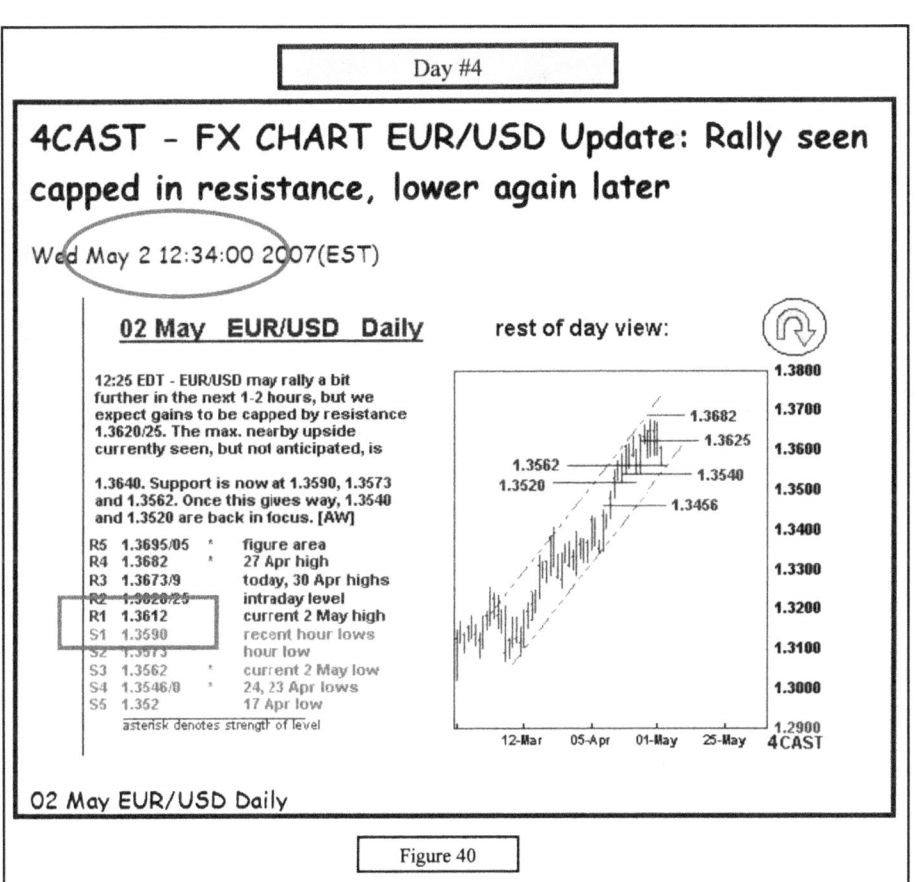

## 4CAST - FX CHART EUR/USD Update: Rally seen capped in resistance, lower again later

Wed May 2 12:34:00 2007(EST)

**02 May EUR/USD Daily**          rest of day view:

12:25 EDT - EUR/USD may rally a bit further in the next 1-2 hours, but we expect gains to be capped by resistance 1.3620/25. The max. nearby upside currently seen, but not anticipated, is

1.3640. Support is now at 1.3590, 1.3573 and 1.3562. Once this gives way, 1.3540 and 1.3520 are back in focus. [AW]

| R5 | 1.3695/05 | * | figure area |
| R4 | 1.3682 | * | 27 Apr high |
| R3 | 1.3673/9 | | today, 30 Apr highs |
| R2 | 1.3620/25 | | intraday level |
| R1 | 1.3612 | | current 2 May high |
| S1 | 1.3590 | | recent hour lows |
| S2 | 1.3573 | | hour low |
| S3 | 1.3562 | * | current 2 May low |
| S4 | 1.3546/0 | * | 24, 23 Apr lows |
| S5 | 1.352 | | 17 Apr low |

asterisk denotes strength of level

02 May EUR/USD Daily

Figure 40

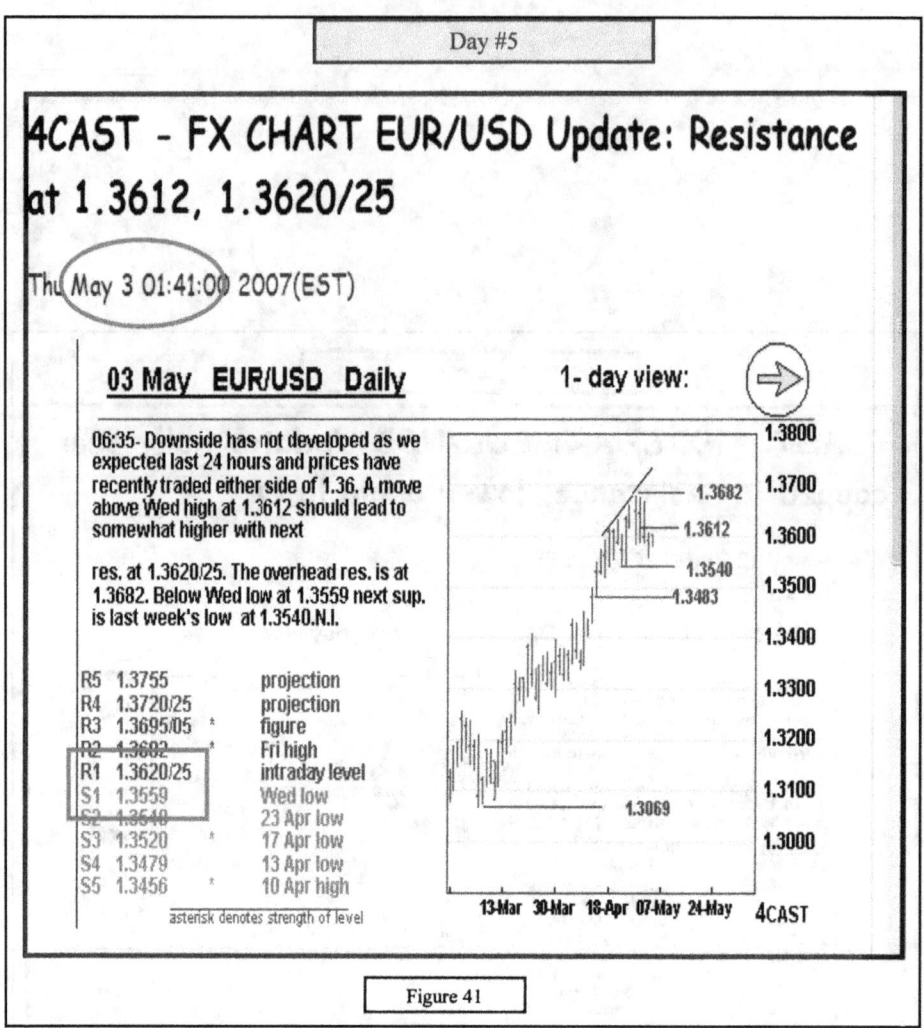

Figure 41

It is important to trade, *in the direction of the news* . If the forecast calls for a weaker EUR, and your trend lines support the conclusion, then concentrate on entering a SELL trade. If it calls for a rise in price, concentrate on entering a BUY trade. *Follow the NEWS!*

*"Do not trade"* when important economic data is coming out. This is to avoid, wild swings in the FOREX market. A check of the news will inform you when important information is going to be released, and the time of its release. FX news, financial networks or the CNBC internet site, will report when important information will be released.

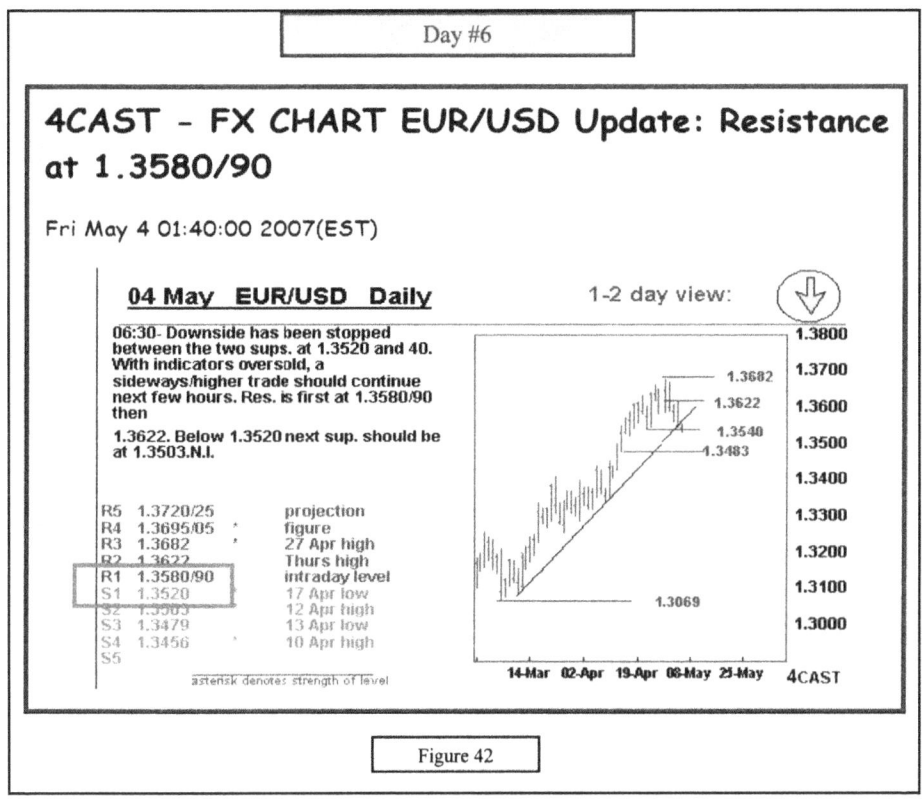

Figure 42

Figure 43, will illustrate a 3 Hour Price Chart, and time frames. Plotted on the chart are the support, and resistance levels, (1), for each of the 6 days.

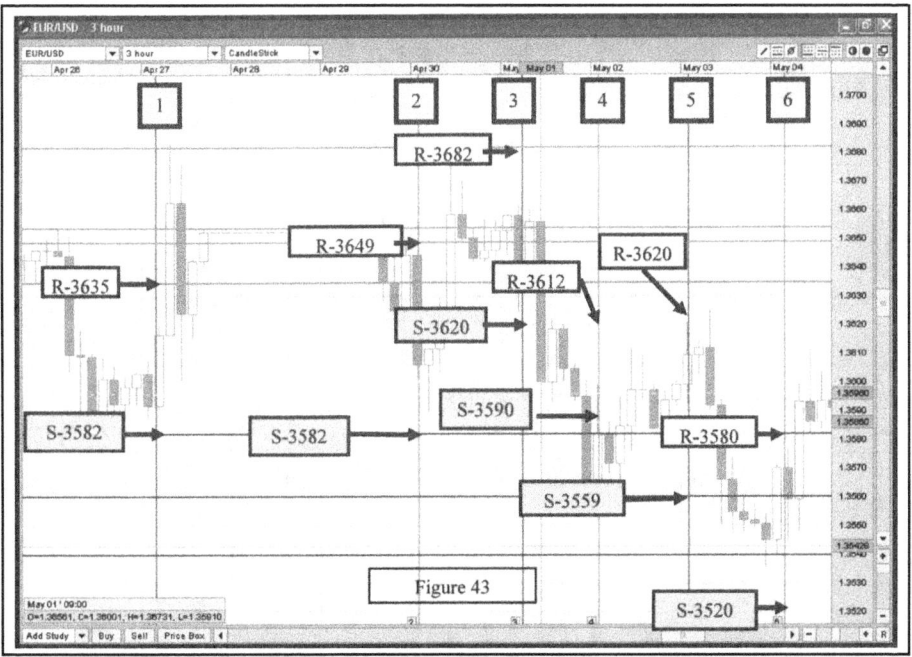

Figure 43

We used the Sell account and placed the listed orders.

We used S-1, first level, of support, and entered a Sell orders, 6 PIPs <u>below</u>, and an Exit, Take Profit, orders at 10 PIPs, further <u>below</u>, the entry point. Results, $30.00 profit. Three orders were never executed.

| Figure 44 | S-1 | Sell Order Entered | Exit Order | Profit/Loss | |
|-----------|-----|--------------------|------------|-------------|---|
| April 27 | 3582 | 3576 | 3566 | No Trade | 0 |
| April 30 | 3582 | 3576 | 3566 | No Trade | 0 |
| May 1 | 3620 | 3614 | 3604 | P—10 PIPS | $10 |
| May 2 | 3590 | 3584 | 3574 | P—10 PIPS | $10 |
| May 3 | 3559 | 3553 | 3543 | P—10 PIPS | $10 |
| May 4 | 3520 | 3514 | 3504 | No Trade | 0 |

This is our record of Buying the EUR above, the resistance level 1

| | Resistance-1 | Buy Order | Exit Sell | Profit/Loss | |
|---|--------------|-----------|-----------|-------------|---|
| April 27 | 3635 | 3641 | 3651 | 10 PIPS | $10.00 |
| April 30 | 3649 | 3655 | 3665 | 10 PIPS | $10.00 |
| May 1 | 3682 | 3688 | 3698 | No Trade | $00.00 |
| May 2 | 3612 | 3620 | 3630 | No Trade | $00.00 |
| May 3 | 3620 | 3626 | 3636 | - 36 PIPS | -$36.00 Unrealized Loss |
| May 4 | 3580 | 3586 | 3596 | 10 PIPS | $10.00 |

Figure 45

Without doing anything else, but reading the <u>currency news</u> ,we made $30.00 profit, on the Sell side and $30.00 on the Buy side, (if we did not close out, our unrealized loss position).

Since the Euro was on a strong up trend, it would have, and did produce, another $10.00 gain. Even if you closed out your losing position, subtracting $36.00 from $60.00, would have netted $24.00 profit. These are much better odds than a casino would offer.

### Trade Technique

1. Click the news analysis every day.
2. Find R-1 and S-1, in 4CAST news, _FX Chart EUR/USD,_ for each day, Monday through Friday.
3. Place a pre-programmed, Buy Limit Order, in the Buy Account, 15 PIPs <u>above</u>, R-1.
4. Place a pre-programmed, Sell Limit Order, in the sell account, 15 PIPs <u>below</u>, S-1.
5. Purchase 10,000 virtual units, for each order.
6. Check, the Take Profit box, when placing orders, 9 PIPs above the entry price, for Buy orders, and 9 PIPs below, the entry price, for Sell orders.
7. Set the Stop Loss Limit at 30 PIPs, then experiment with 15 PIPs, and 25 PIPs. Check your results.
8. Do this each day, for the next 30 days.

For easy trading, program your user preference. Click open Trading and set the Stop Lost to 30 PIPs And your Take Profit to 9 PIPs.

I believe that you can produce profits if you use the <u>news technique</u>.

This method of trading can fit a busy schedule.

# MOVING AVERAGES

Here is a simple yet powerful trading indicator, to help you make winning trades.

As you have seen from currency price charts, prices move up, and down by the second. A moving average line smoothes out closing prices over a period of time and charts it for you. This allows traders to see the currency trend. Simply put, a 10 day moving average is the product of adding up 10 days of closing prices and dividing it by 10. This calculation is then visually plotted for you on the currency chart. On the 11th day, the first day is removed, and the information is recalculated.

Moving average days can be displayed as you wish—2, 7, 14, 30, 50, 100, 150, and 200 days.

There are three types of moving averages. We will use the *Exponential Moving Average* in our trades. Using a complicated math formula, the EMA gives greater weight, to the *latest closing prices*, and instantly displays the information on your computer. You can read detailed information on different types of moving averages at, investopedia.com.

Moving average lines can signal when to enter or exit a trade. It can reveal support for a currency's price, or resistance to further price increase. When the price line falls below the moving average line, the currency is headed down. If the prices move up, through the EMA, it signals further price increase.

One action is certain, the price line will return to the EMA line. You will see this action repeat itself over and over again.

This section will cover the use of:

- Single EMA line
- Multiple EMA lines
- Active trading using two EMA lines.

Figure 46, displays a 100 Day, EMA line, plotted on the *Day, Price Chart.*

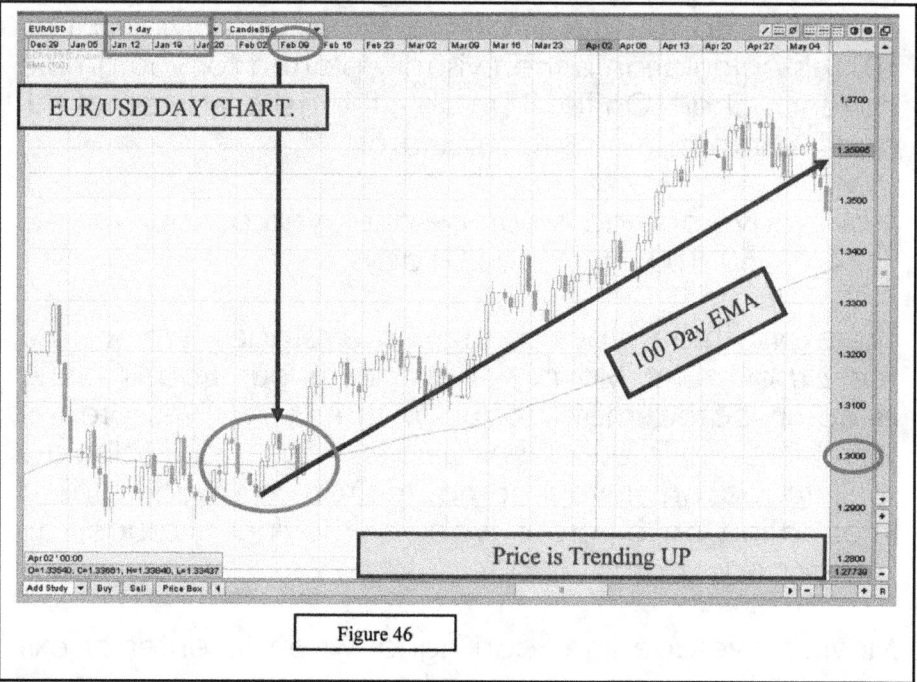

Figure 46

Assume a BUY order was entered on Feb. 9th., 2007, for 10,000 units, at the price of 1.3000. The Euro continued to rise in value and peaked out in April. Notice that the price broke down past the *Trend Line*. The *Trend line* break out was the first signal to exit, at a price of 1.3500. For this study, let us assume that we waited until the price passed down, through the 100 day EMA line, on May 7th., 2007. If the trade had been closed out, at the sale price of, 1.3370, it would have resulted in 370 PIPs gained.

10,000 units at $1.00 per PIP, would equal, $370.00. As the chart shows, the price line will move away from the moving average line, but eventually returns, and crosses it. The cross over points are the signals, to either BUY or SELL a currency. Longer term trading is the easiest and safest way to trade. Short term is exciting, fast, but generally not as profitable.

For *training*, we practice short term trading, to gain experience.

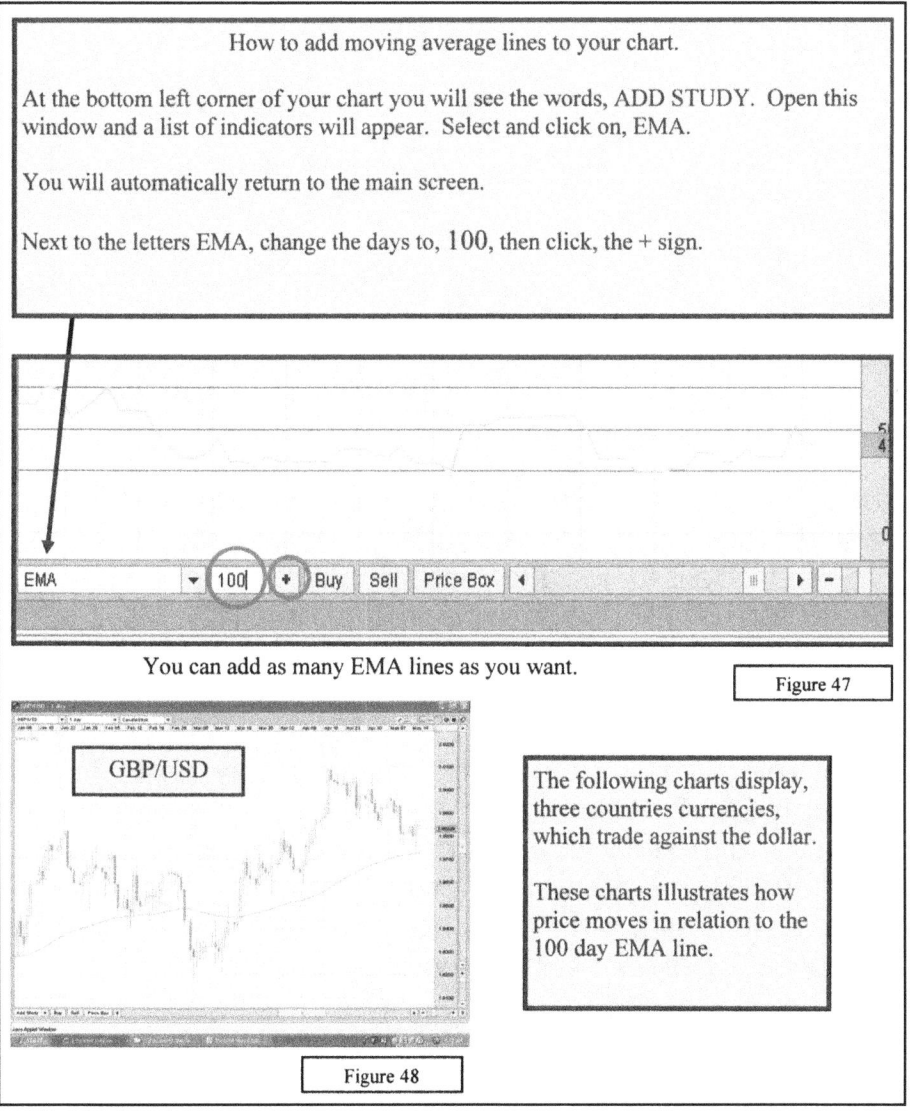

How to add moving average lines to your chart.

At the bottom left corner of your chart you will see the words, ADD STUDY. Open this window and a list of indicators will appear. Select and click on, EMA.

You will automatically return to the main screen.

Next to the letters EMA, change the days to, 100, then click, the + sign.

EMA    100    +    Buy    Sell    Price Box

You can add as many EMA lines as you want.

Figure 47

GBP/USD

The following charts display, three countries currencies, which trade against the dollar.

These charts illustrates how price moves in relation to the 100 day EMA line.

Figure 48

USD/CAD

Figure 49

AUD/USD

Figure 50

*"Trade Technique"*

If you have a busy schedule you can view the 6 major currencies once a day.

Using the *Day Chart*, when a price reaches the , 100 day, EMA line, enter a BUY order in the primary account and SELL order in the sub-account, 15 PIPS distance, from the line.

Exit target will be, 19 PIPS, take profit. To your *entry price* add, 19 PIPS, on a BUY order, and subtract, 19 PIPS, on the SELL order.

On a strong up trend or down trend, keep your trade open, until a reversal occurs.

Since this is practice, trade cross currencies such as the EUR/JYP.

You can also do this trade on the shorter time frame charts.

Using the *15 minute chart*, reduce your entry distance to 6 Pips, from the line. Exit the trade by taking profit at 4 Pips.

Using the Day Chart is not a complicated trade and requires looking at the chart a few minutes each day. This type of trade is for long term trading. Your stop loss should be set for 100 PIPs, your expected gain is 100 PIPs. If your gain is expected to be 50 PIPs your stop loss should be 50 PIPs. The 50% rule is basic money management system.

By keeping losses at a minimum, you only need to be correct 50% of the time to stay profitable. In the beginning, while using the practice account, stop loss need not be a concern. As you gain experience, begin to religiously use the stop loss rule. When you have mastered the stop loss discipline, open a real money account.

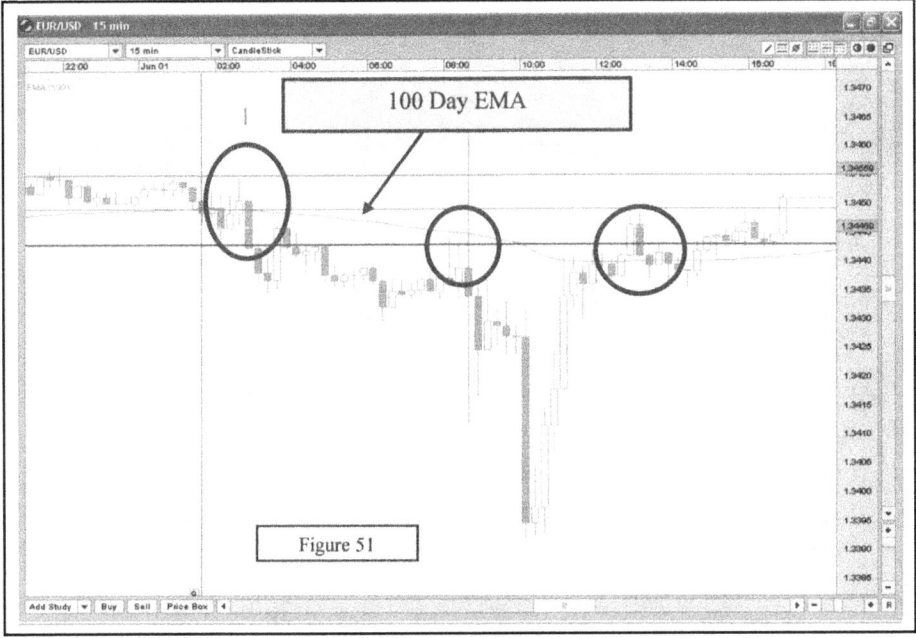

Figure 51

Figure 51 shows the *15 minute* chart, with the 100 Day EMA line displayed. Using the trade technique previously covered, a *6 Pip entry*, and a *4 Pip exit*, you would have been profitable, at all three circles.

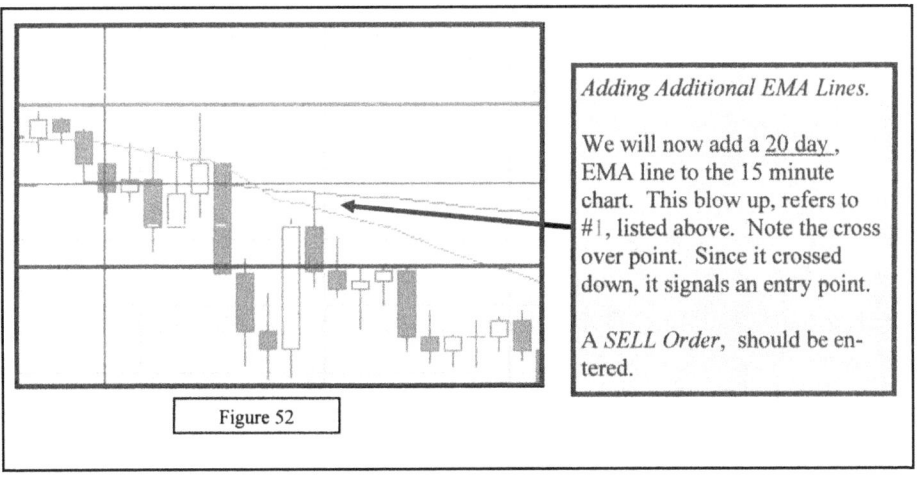

*Adding Additional EMA Lines.*

We will now add a 20 day, EMA line to the 15 minute chart. This blow up, refers to #1, listed above. Note the cross over point. Since it crossed down, it signals an entry point.

A *SELL Order*, should be entered.

Figure 52

## Multiple Moving Average Lines

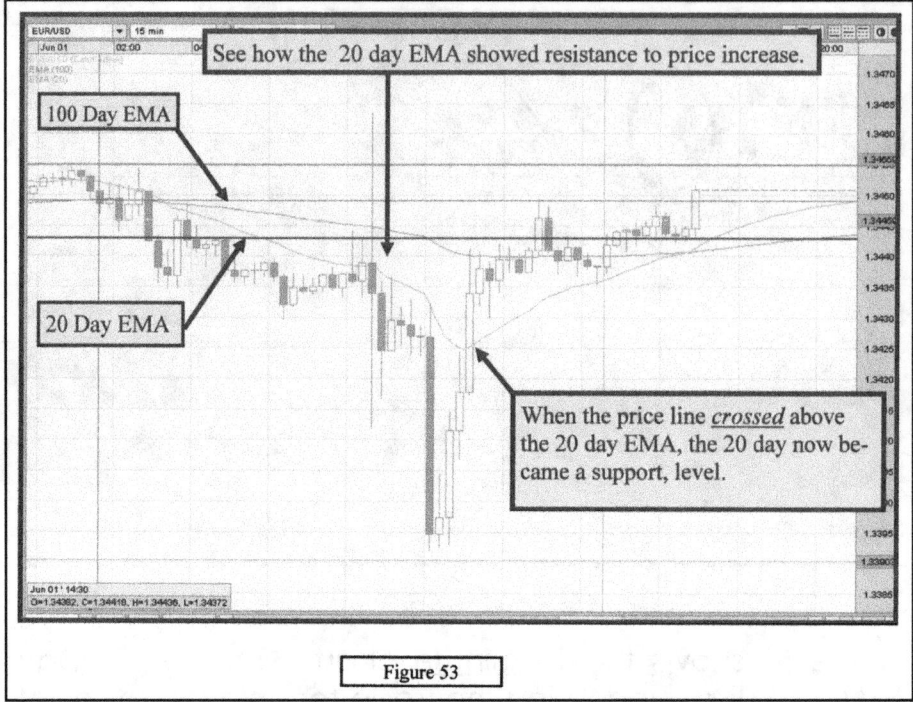

Figure 53

Figure 54 displays multiple EMA lines, to determine *changing* support and resistance levels. The 2, 5, 14, 30, 50, 100, 150, and 200 day EMA lines are displayed. Notice how each price crossing, *downward*, causes the next level to be possible support. Price drop finally stops at the 100 day line. We are looking for price support and a trend reversal.

Notice how the EMA lines began to compress. As the lines merge, a price reversal will result. For long term trading, we want to determine either the final support or resistance level. Once this is established, a price reversal results.

On the following pages we will use two moving average lines, for short term, active trading. The coming lessons will give you the opportunity to enter and exit trades frequently. We will do this to give you practice, using the trading platform.

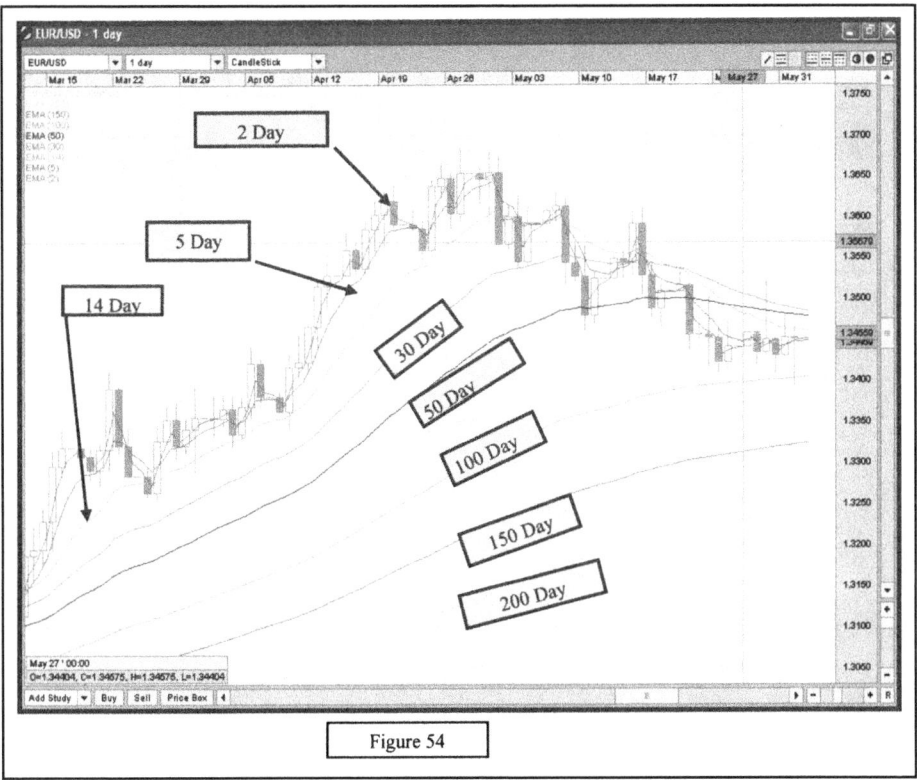

Figure 54

We will use only one account until you become proficient in trading.

# TRADING MOVING AVERAGES

Look at your News information and read what the experts predict for the, EUR/USD. We will concentrate on trading in the direction of the trend. If the experts say we should be buying, we will concentrate on buying opportunities. If they say the Euro looks weak or bearish, we would be selling.

Before the trade, the 15 minute chart should be viewed, to obtain a longer term view of the price movement. Is the price rising or falling?

Trading will entail the use of the 5 minute, 1 minute, and 30 second chart.

Two EMA lines will be added to the chart, the 30 day, and the 5 day, EMA lines.

Our goal is to observe the 30 second chart. When the 5 day EMA, crosses up through the 30 day EMA, switch to the 1 minute chart. Observe the 5 day EMA, on the 1 minute chart. When the 5 day EMA, crosses up, through the 30 day EMA line, enter a 10,000 unit, Buy order. It is a good rule to wait until two full candlesticks are displayed.

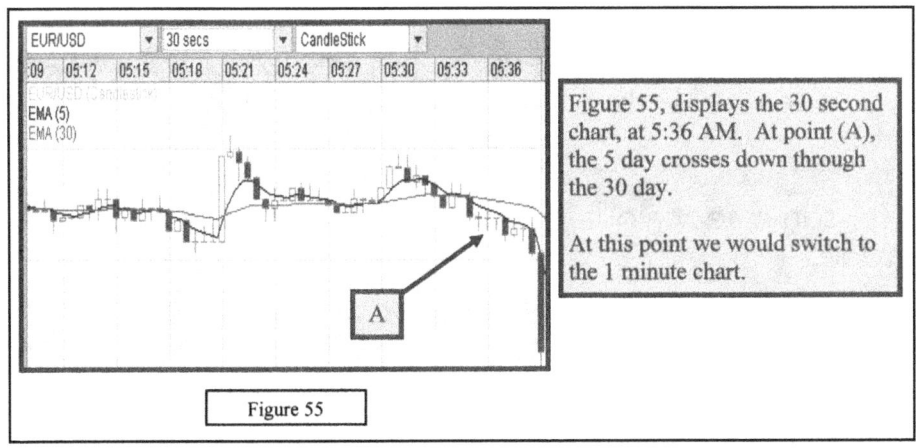

Figure 55, displays the 30 second chart, at 5:36 AM. At point (A), the 5 day crosses down through the 30 day.

At this point we would switch to the 1 minute chart.

Figure 55

71

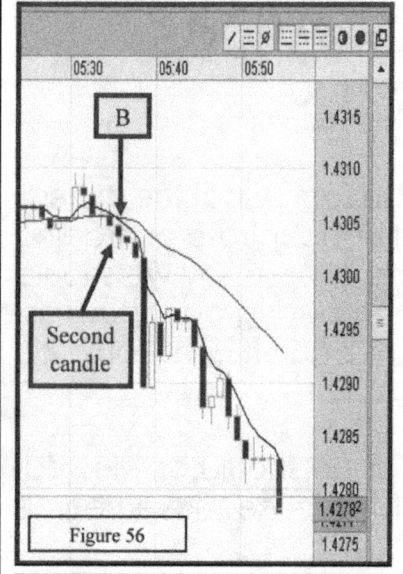

Figure 56, the 1 minute chart. At 5:38AM, point (B), the 5 day EMA, crosses down through the 30 day EMA.

We would wait for two full candlesticks, then enter a 10,000 unit, sell order.

Exit the trade when the 5 day, turns up.

Figure 57, shows the 5 minute chart. Notice how the 5 day EMA line, does not touch the 30 day line.

With the trend lines drawn, one would exit the trade, when the price line moved up through the resistance trend line.

Figure 56

Figure 57

Switch back to the 30 second, or 10 second chart. When you see the 5 day EMA, reverse downward, exit the trade.

The same technique applies if we were entering a Sell trade.

# RELATIVE STRENGTH INDICATOR

Relative strength indicator is an oscillator. It is an <u>excellent indicator</u> of BUY and SELL signals. It moves between 100, upper limit, to 0, at the lower limit. The indicator compares the number of <u>up</u> days of a currency, to the number of days, the price was <u>lower</u>. The time frame covers 14 days.

When the RSI reaches the 70% level, it is considered <u>overbought</u>. When the line reaches the 30% level, it is considered <u>oversold</u>. "See glossary of terms."

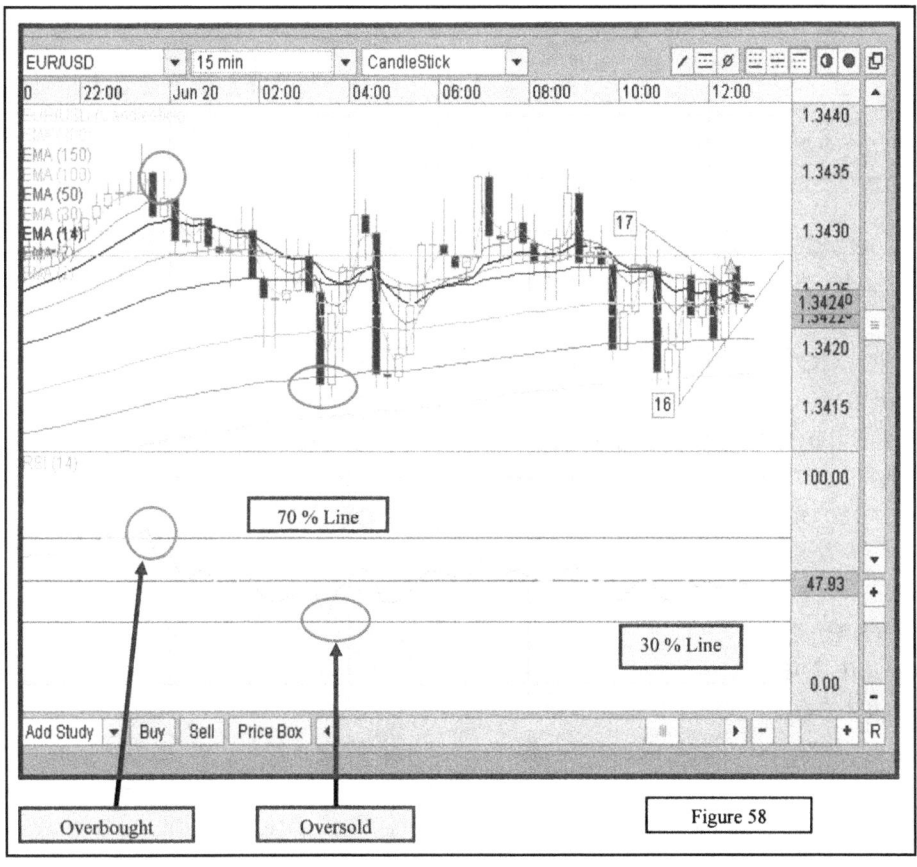

Figure 58

73

Figure 59

The dashed line displayed in figure 59 indicates the middle of the RSI indicator, which has a value of 50%.

Notice how the RSI is below the 50% line, as compared to being above it. This indicates a down trend for the EUR. The price line confirms this. You would enter, *sell orders*, when the price increases, (*rallies up*). Your SELL Order is entered when the RSI reaches, or passes the 70% line.

View the price chart. Observe that the EUR price line, never crossed above the 50 day, EMA line. This indicates that the 50 Day, EMA line, is a barrier, (*resistance*), to further price increases.

If you view the RSI, on the DAY Chart, you will see how accurate this indicator is. When the price approaches the 70% or the 30% RSI, a price reversal will soon follow.

Generally, if a Sell order is entered, at the overbought price, and the trade is Exited, at the oversold point, a profit will result. If a Buy order is entered, at the oversold line, and the trade is closed out when the RSI reached 50%, or higher, a profit would have also resulted. Figure 60, shown below, visually depicts resistance to higher prices or support for price. Traders are constantly changing positions from buyers to sellers, and vice versa. While you are reading this book, 3 trillion dollars are changing hands, 24 hours per day. It boggles the mind, that every second, money is being bought and sold, six days a week.

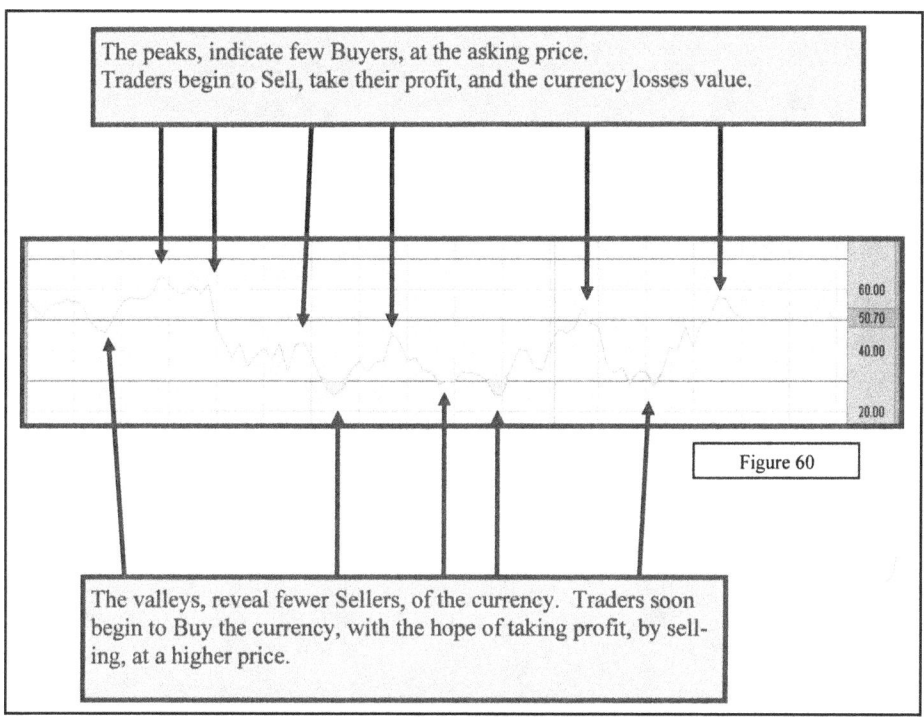

The peaks, indicate few Buyers, at the asking price.
Traders begin to Sell, take their profit, and the currency losses value.

60.00
50.70
40.00
20.00

Figure 60

The valleys, reveal fewer Sellers, of the currency. Traders soon begin to Buy the currency, with the hope of taking profit, by selling, at a higher price.

The most powerful *Buy or Sell signals* are displayed on longer time frame charts. Observe what happens when the price reaches, 70% or higher, or nears the 30% line. A price reversal will soon follow.

This indicator is **NOT VALID**, during crisis in government or unexpected news shocks. Such events cause the indicator to move to extreme levels.

# TRADING THE RSI

As always, one would read the FX currency trading briefs, for the EUR/USD.

At the time of this writing, the news indicated, that the market was choppy, and the Euro, would attempt to reach 1.4350.

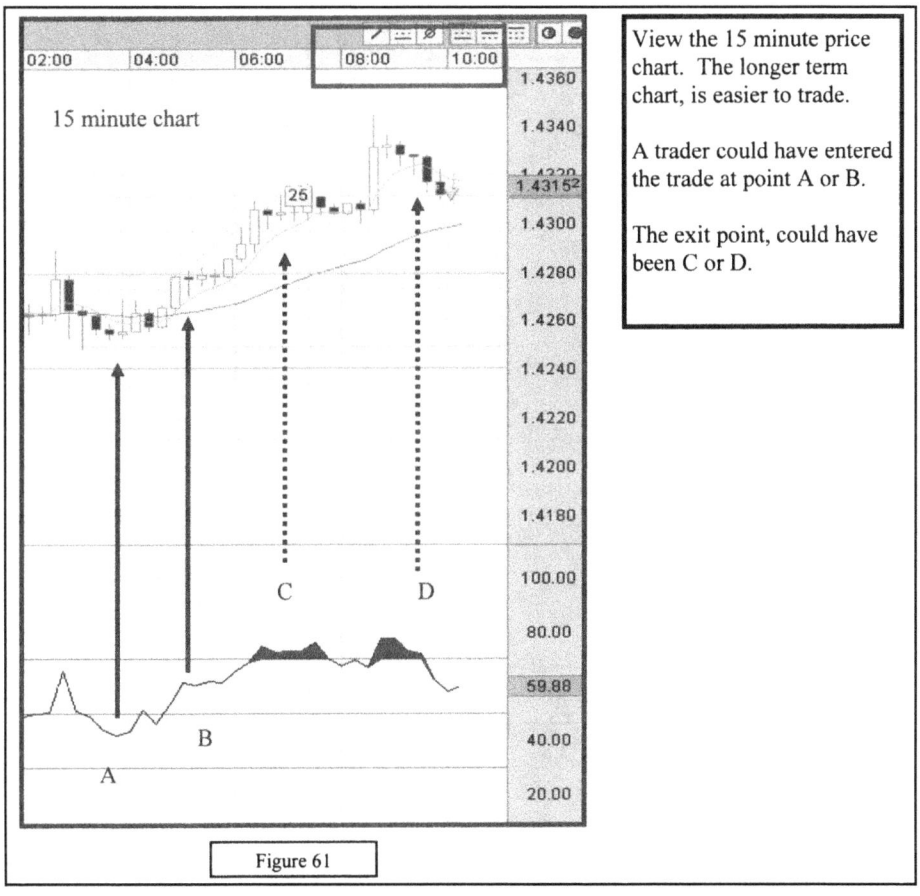

View the 15 minute price chart. The longer term chart, is easier to trade.

A trader could have entered the trade at point A or B.

The exit point, could have been C or D.

Figure 61

The following charts will cover a time period from 8:00AM, through 10AM.

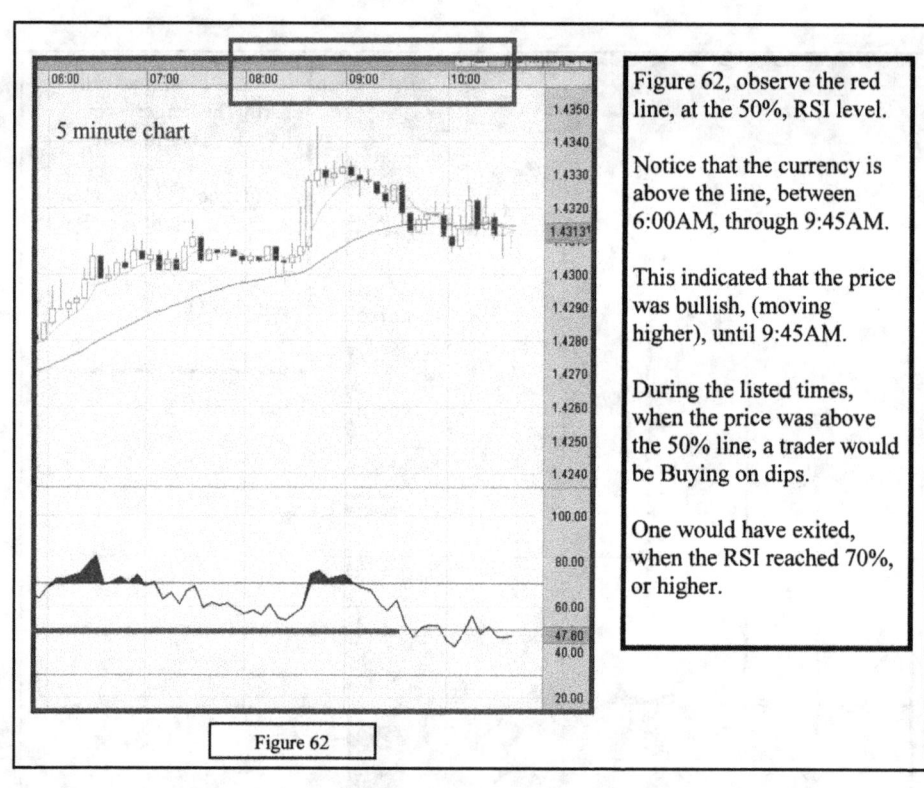

5 minute chart

Figure 62, observe the red line, at the 50%, RSI level.

Notice that the currency is above the line, between 6:00AM, through 9:45AM.

This indicated that the price was bullish, (moving higher), until 9:45AM.

During the listed times, when the price was above the 50% line, a trader would be Buying on dips.

One would have exited, when the RSI reached 70%, or higher.

Figure 62

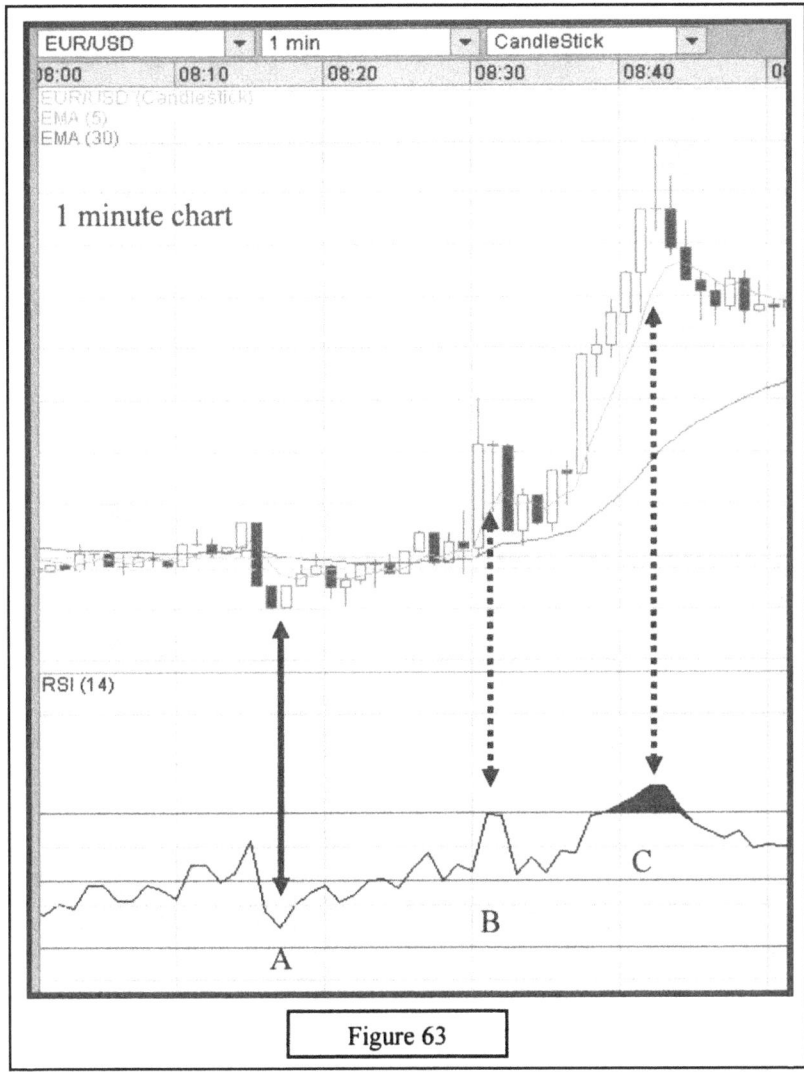

EUR/USD    1 min    CandleStick

08:00   08:10   08:20   08:30   08:40   0

EUR/USD (CandleStick)
EMA (5)
EMA (30)

1 minute chart

RSI (14)

C

B

A

Figure 63

The 1 minute chart allows a, minute by minute, view of the trading activity. From 8:10AM, through 8:45AM, a trader could have entered a buy trade, at point (A), and exited, at point, (B) or (C).

In this section we are showing the RSI entry points only. The best entry point is the combination of the moving average crossover and the RSI rising.

In this section, we will only use the RSI indicator. As you gain experience you will combine indicators.

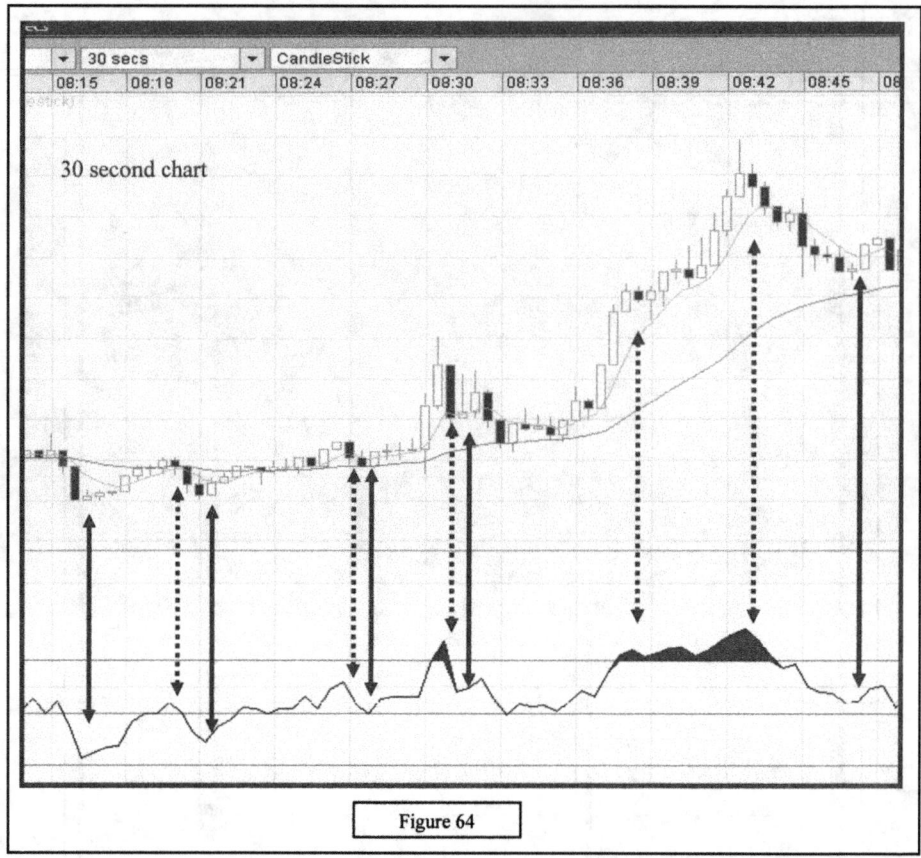

Figure 64

The 30 second chart is for very active trading. Each candlestick represents the price movement during a 30 second period of time. I recommend trading this chart for practice only.

The solid black lines would be the entry points, and the dashed lines would be the exit points.

The trade from start to finish, will take less than five minutes.

# ADDING THE RSI

You can access the RSI indicator and place it on your chart by clicking on, ADD STUDY.

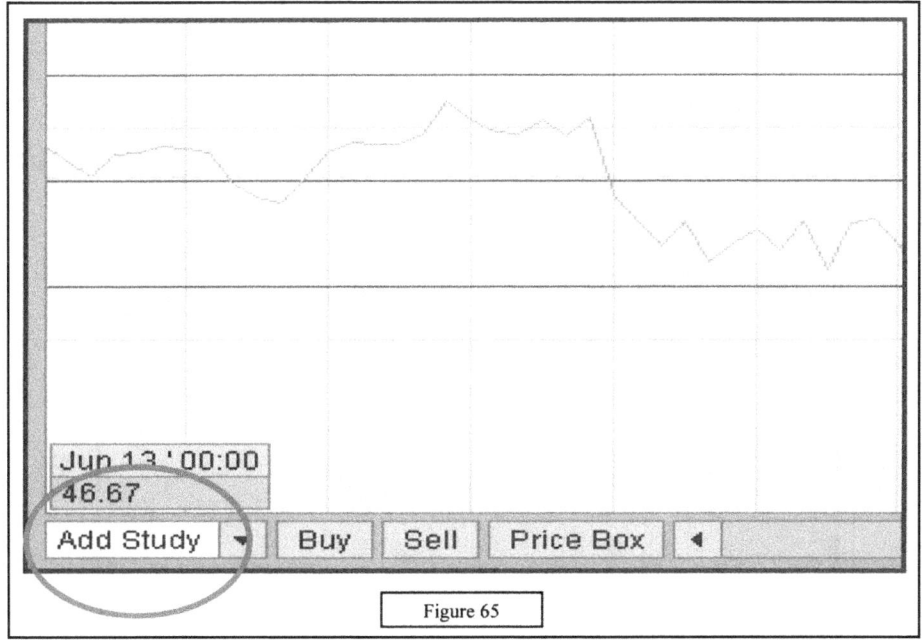

Figure 65

When the window opens, locate the letters, RSI, and click on it.

After window closes, click the (+) sign button, and the RSI will appear below the chart as shown in figure 65.

## Trading Technique, Using the RSI

Our goal is to use the RSI indicator, to pre-program, six Buy Orders. We will use three charts, the 15 minute, 5 minute, and 1 minute chart.

The following information will help you determine your entry point.

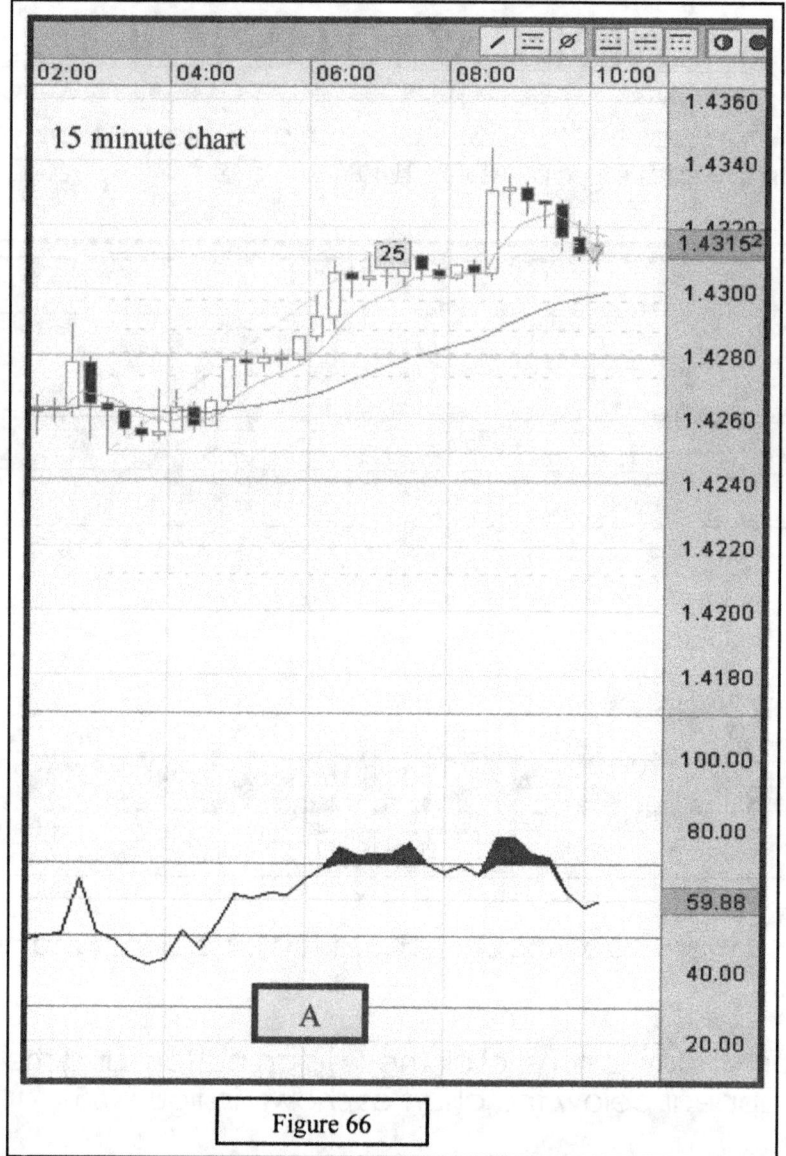

Figure 66

Open the 15 minute chart and check the news.

Assume the news stated the Euro was projected to increase in value, to $1.4400.

Place your mouse cursor in the RSI area of the chart, (A), and left click the mouse.

A dialog box will open, and the words, Horizontal Line, will appear. Click, on horizontal line.

The line will appear in the RSI box. As you move the mouse, the line will move also. It is important to keep this line within the RSI area.

Place this line on the 30% line, but do not click your mouse. In Oanda's trading platform, a second line will be displayed in the price chart area. This line follows the up, or down movement of the RSI, horizontal line.

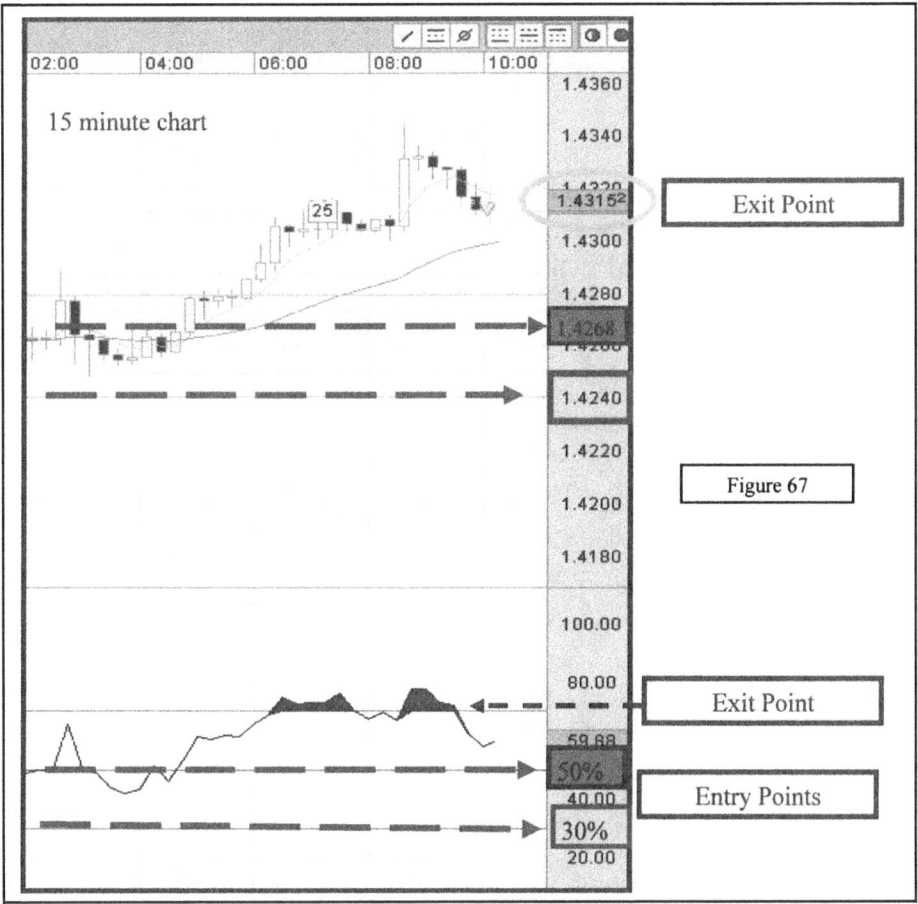

With the horizontal line positioned at the 30%, RSI level, a second, parallel line will be displayed above, on the price chart. Shown, on the far right side of the line will be the price, 1.4240. This will be our 30%, pre-programmed, BUY entry point. We will move the horizontal, RSI line, further up, to the 50% level, and read the second price, 1.4268, as shown on the price chart. Move the horizontal, RSI line, up to the 70% level. The price of 1.4315.2 is the exit point of the trade.

Write down all three numbers, Buy at 1.4240, Buy at 1.4268, and Exit at 1.4315.2. Repeat these steps for the 5 minute, and 30 second chart.

We Buy if the news says to Buy on dips, or we enter Sell Orders, if the news says to sell.

Use the *full chart* display screen to obtain your prices. Since the FOREX is a fluid market, you should recheck, your entry and exit points every hour, if possible. If you do recheck the RSI values you will find that they change more for the 30 second chart and a little for the 5 minute chart.

Your order would look like figure 68. Click on, Limit Order, purchase 10,000 units, at 1.4240, and your Take Profit would be set at, 1.4315. For training, do not check the stop loss. You can also, manually, take profit, when you want. If you take profit re-enter your previous order.

If you like, you can set your stop loss, at the price given in the FX news, currency trading brief.

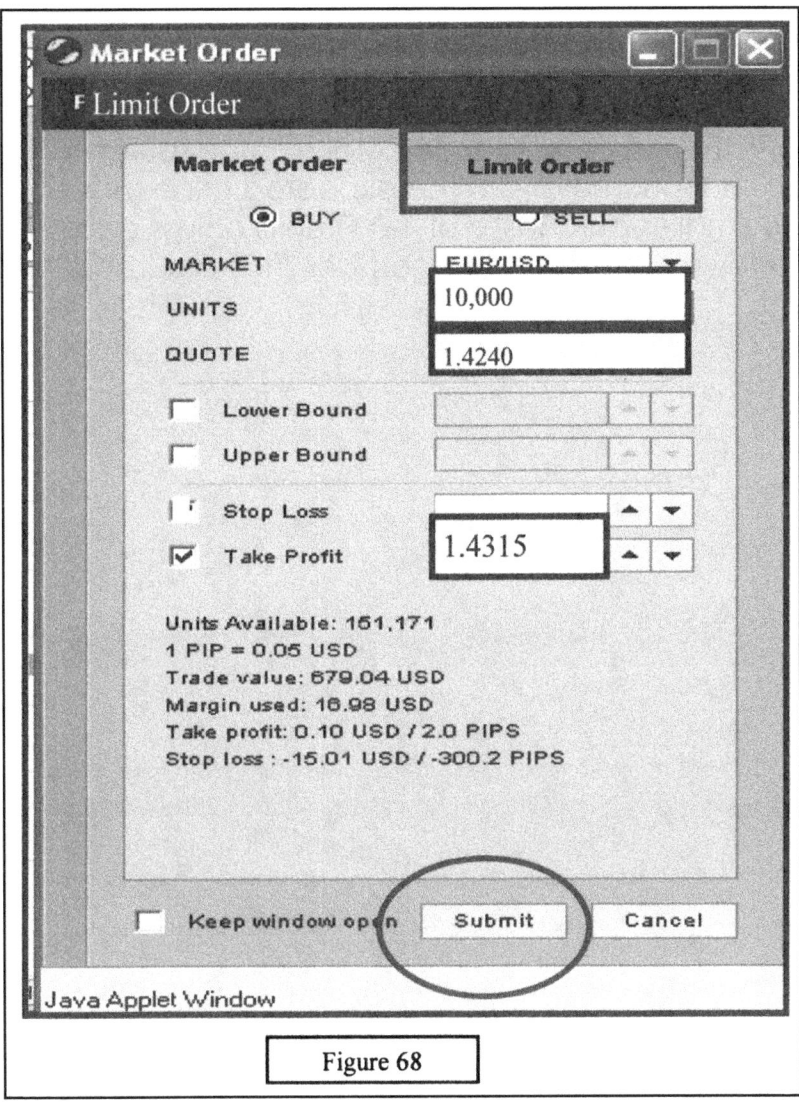

Figure 68

If the news predicts a price drop for the currency, use the same steps in reverse. Place a sell order for the 70% level and 50% level price. Exit your trade at the 30% level price, of 1.4240.

It will be easier to record your entry and exit prices on a sheet of paper, then enter them as Limit Orders.

You can work both sides of the trade by using your two accounts. In your BUY account use the 30% and 50% entry point. In your SELL account use the 70% and 50% prices as entry points.

Follow the news guidance. Make large purchases, of 10,000 units or more with the expected price movement. Make smaller purchases of 1,000 units or less against the currency trend. Always remember that the trend is your friend.

# PUTTING IT TOGETHER

Traders use a combination of indicators to make trades.

- Determine the long term trend, using the day chart and three hour chart.
- On the Day chart, *draw,* your support and resistance, trend lines.
- Add to the Chart the following EMA, moving average lines: 30 day EMA, and the 5 day EMA. As you zoom in on the different chart, time frames, the EMA lines will automatically adjust.
- Add the RSI indicator, and view the long term chart time frames. Is the currency closer to 70% or 30%?
- Enter pre-programmed RSI, entry and exit orders.
- If you have limited time, use the Day Chart, 3 hour, and one hour Chart combinations. Determine your preprogrammed entry and exit points, using the RSI formula.

Your decision to enter and exit a trade will be based on the following indicators:

- The NEWS.
- Trend Line break out points.
- The moving average crossover points.
- Support and or Resistance levels, as given in the News.
- The 70% and 30%, RSI levels.

Technical indicators have a self fulfilling life to them. Since so many people use and follow them, a herd mentality results. When many people see certain signs or breakouts, they react as a group, and move in the same direction.

Experiment by opening two additional sub-accounts. Name the accounts, News-Buy, and News-Sell. Practice placing orders in these accounts "just" using the news technique.

Pre-program your entry, SELL or BUY, orders, based on the support and resistance level #1, as given in, 4CAST news.

Trade the guidance given by, Thompson Financial, news trading briefs. Thompson Financial uses the following abbreviations:

- O/B...........over bought.
- Flat.........close out the trade if price does not exceed this price level.
- SELL.......enter a sell order at this price.
- LONG......place a buy order at this price.
- SHORT....be ready to enter a sell order.

The narrative given by Thompson's will help explain the trade details.

The news guidance and the three indicators covered in this book, will give you sufficient information to trade the market.

If you feel confused, use one technique only, and practice trading. I recommend you practice for at least three months, before opening a "real money" account. You are learning a new skill, and with practice you will gain confidence.

The advantages of FOREX TRADING are many.

You can learn and practice without risking capital.

You can measure your results.

Family members can compete, using multiple sub-accounts. This can be an exciting and educational experience.

Real money trading requires very little investment capital, yet can produce a good return.

Unlike stocks, you do not need to know about a company's financial strength.

You have a 24 hour trading window, which will fit any schedule.

# GLOSSARY OF TERMS

Bank of Japan—BOJ, central bank of Japan.

Bear Market—trader who believes prices will fall.

Bundesbank—the central bank of Germany.

Buying On Margin—taking a position in a currency when only a portion of the total value is paid for. The rest is borrowed and interest is charged. The portion paid for is called margin.

Central Bank—a country's main bank, monitored by its government, whose role is to regulate other banks and financial institutions, and to enact monetary policy.

Candlestick Chart—a chart used for technical analysis purposes, made popular by Japanese rice merchants to track the price of rice over time.

Carry—the cost of keeping a position open overnight. Each currency has a different interest rate associated with it. You are *paid interest* on the currency you are long in, and must pay interest on the currency you are short. The difference is the carry or is sometimes referred to as the cost of carry.

Central Bank Intervention—when the central bank enters the spot forex market to buy or sell forex in order to stabilize the country's currency, usually when supply or demand forces are unbalanced.

Cross Currency Contract—a contract to buy or sell one foreign currency in exchange for another foreign currency, neither of which involves the US Dollar.

Congestion— A period of time where a currency trades below resistance and above Support, for a period of time, sideways movement.

European Central Bank—ECB, the central bank of the European Monetary Union.

Easing—refers to either a small price decline in a currency or when a central bank engages in lowering interest rates to spur spending.

Factory Orders—an economic indicator which measures the change from one period to another for orders for durable and nondurable goods. More orders mean growth whereas the opposite signifies a slowdown.

Fundamental Analysis—analysis of political and economic information with the objective of determining future movements in the financial markets.

Foreign Exchange—buying or selling one currency against another currency.

Foreign Exchange Centers—the largest forex center in the world is London. Other financial centers which follow the sun across the sky are New York, Tokyo, Hong Kong, Singapore, and Zurich. Trading passes from one center to the next, the traders in one bank desk handing off the trading book to their colleagues in another center.

Fed Fund Rate—the interest rate on Fed fund account balances which is closely monitored to gauge the Fed's view on the economy. The accounts are held by member banks and are usually used for lending or borrowing from one another.

G7—the seven leading industrialized countries: Canada, France, Germany, Italy, Japan, the United Kingdom, and the United States of America.

Golden Cross—in technical analysis, when two moving averages intersect, usually a short one like a 20 day and a long one such as 40 day. This is considered a favorable sign that the underlying currency will move in the same direction.

Head And Shoulders—A price trend pattern which has three peaks, the middle one higher than the surrounding two forming what looks to be a head with two shoulders on either side. This pattern is seen as an indicator of a trend reversal.

Leverage—the ratio of margin to the maximum position size. With a deposit of $5000 and a leverage of 50, a trader could enter a position with a face value of $250,000. Leveraging allows you to profit quickly, but lose money just as quickly.

Limit Order—an order to transact at a specified price or better.

Liquid—Term used to describe a market where there are lots of buyers and sellers generating much volume.

Liquidation—this is what happens as a result of a margin call. All positions are closed to prevent further loss. At margin call, the value of the account is not sufficient to sustain the position size.

Moving Average—a method of smoothing out data on price charts, so that trends are easier to spot. Average refers to a mathematical average or a statistical "mean" that is plotted over the original curve.

M1 - Money supply component which consists of all cash in circulation, plus all of the money held in checking accounts, as well as all the money in travelers checks.

M2— Money supply component which consists of M1 plus all of the money held in money market funds, savings accounts and small Certificates of Deposits.

M3— Money supply component which consists of M2 plus all of the large Certificates of Deposits.

Over bought—the price of an asset is overvalued and may present a pull back in price.

Over sold—where the price of an asset has fallen and is now considered undervalued.

Political Risk—Changes in government policy or to a wider extent, government instability that might have negative effects on the currency.

Regulated Market—A market in which a government agency monitors and regulates industry activity to protect investors. An example is forex trading in the United States.

Resistance—a ceiling at which price isn't able to penetrate, because of high selling activity.

Sell Limit Order—an order to enter a position only at a specified price (the limit) or higher. FXTrade limit orders are executed as soon as the market price reaches the quote.

Selling Short—selling a currency pair that involves being short the base currency and long the quote currency, with the intent of profiting by buying the currency pair at a lower price.

Stop Loss Order—a limit order to close a position when a given limit is reached. When long, the stop loss order is placed below the current market price. When short, the stop loss order is placed above the current market price.

Take Profit Order—a limit order that is placed above the market with a long position or below the market with a short position. When the markets reach the limit price, the position is closed, thereby locking in a profit.

Technical Analysis—Use of historical rates, price charts, and other market data to forecast future prices.

Trend—the current direction of the market, whether up or down or sideways (which is sometimes referred to as non-trending or trading market).

Unrealized P/L—the valuation of the current position and the resultant profit or loss if the position were to be liquidated at that moment.

Whipsaw—Refers to when a position is taken and a stop loss is created. The market moves down to trigger the stop loss and then turns around. In this way, the trader suffers two losses. The loss associated with the stop loss which was put below the position's entry level and the loss of not being able to participate in the subsequent rise of the currency pair.

Additional definition of terms can be found on the following web site: investopedia.com

# ABOUT THE AUTHOR

Harry Cunill is a licensed real estate and mortgage broker. He operates his own company, Sunpass Realty, located in Miami, Florida. He served as a sergeant for the City of Miami Police and retired from the Miami Springs Police Department. He resides on beautiful Marco Island, Florida.